Phonics
Made Simple
····················

Grade 2

Written by Vicky Shiotsu
Illustrated by Jenny Campbell
and Becky Radtke

FS123308 Phonics Made Simple—Grade 2
All rights reserved–Printed in the U.S.A.
Copyright © 2000 Frank Schaffer Publications, Inc.
23740 Hawthorne Blvd.
Torrance, CA 90505

Editor: Jeanine Manfro
Art Director: Anthony Paular
Graphic Artist: Randy Shinsato

Table
of Contents

Introduction

Phonics is an important tool for understanding how written English "works." As children learn about the relationship between sounds and letters, they see that how a word is read or written is based on certain systematic rules.

Many consonants make only one sound.

Some consonants can be grouped to form new sounds.

The sounds of vowels vary.

Learning phonics is an important key in learning how to read and write.

Reading and writing are essential skills of communication. An important part of acquiring these skills comes from a knowledge of phonetic rules and an understanding of how written English "works." *Phonics Made Simple—Grade 2* is designed to help teachers plan a phonics program that helps children become aware of the relationship between the letters of the alphabet and the sounds of English. The activities in this book incorporate a variety of sensory experiences—visual aids, movement activities, poems, creative writing, and more—to make learning phonics both stimulating and rewarding. As students develop the ability to discriminate consonant and vowel sounds, they gain the skills needed to read and write words on their own. These early successes in reading and writing are crucial in the development of a child's self-confidence and self-esteem, and they lay the foundation for future learning.

Phonics Made Simple—Grade 2 can be used alone or as an integral part of any language arts program. The book is divided into six sections: *Consonants, Short Vowels, Long Vowels, Consonant Blends and Digraphs, R-Controlled Vowels,* and *Special Vowels.* Each section presents a variety of activities that are interesting, challenging, and age-appropriate. The activities in each section may be introduced sequentially as they appear in the book or in random order.

Consonants

CONCEPTS

The ideas and activities presented in this section will help children develop the following skills:

- **identifying beginning, medial, and final consonant sounds**
- **distinguishing between the sounds of two or more consonants**
- **choosing words that have a particular beginning or final consonant**

Distinguishing the sounds of the consonants can be thought of as the "jumping-off" point from which young children begin learning how to read and write. Consonants produce sounds that are more consistent and more easily identifiable than vowels. That is why children are usually taught consonant sounds before vowel sounds. Students entering the second grade already have had a lot of experience working with consonants. A review of consonants at the beginning of the year, though, is useful for assessing children's skills and for identifying the students who need extra reinforcement.

CHECK CONSONANT SOUNDS

Class Activity

Check your students' auditory discrimination of initial and final consonants with this "spelling" test. Give each child a sheet of paper and have the class number the papers from 1 to 33. Then say the following words one at a time, and have the students write the beginning sounds for numbers 1 to 20 and the ending sounds for numbers 21 to 33:

1. **b**ook 2. **f**an 3. **c**at 4. **g**ood 5. **d**uck 6. **h**at 7. **k**ite 8. **y**am 9. **j**ug 10. **z**ebra
11. **n**et 12. **l**amp 13. **m**op 14. **p**ot 15. **r**oad 16. **q**ueen 17. **t**able 18. **s**eal
19. **w**agon 20. **v**iolin 21. tu**b** 22. ra**g** 23. bal**l** 24. sa**d** 25. cu**p** 26. je**t** 27. roo**f**
28. spoo**n** 29. bu**s** 30. hu**m** 31. buz**z** 32. fo**x** 33. loo**k**

Afterwards, check the students' work to see if any child has difficulty distinguishing particular consonants.

Game

Consonant Bingo

Review consonants with this easy game. First, choose words that begin or end with consonants, and write each word on a slip of paper. Place the words in a paper bag. Next, give each student a sheet of paper and some bingo counters (beans, pieces of paper, or other markers). Instruct the students to draw a 4 x 4 grid, and have them write a consonant in each of the 16 spaces. Tell the students that they will be listening for the beginning (or ending) sound. Then draw a slip of paper from the bag and read the word aloud. Ask a student to state the beginning or ending consonant, and then have the children look to see if they have the letter. If they do, have them place a counter on it. Continue the procedure with other words. The first student to get four letters in a row wins.

FS123308 Phonics Made Simple—Grade 2 ■ © Frank Schaffer Publications, Inc.

WORD CHALLENGE

Let your students work in pairs for this challenging word activity. Write two consonants on the board and draw a line between them (example: *c___t*). Then challenge the students to write as many words as they can that begin and end with the consonants you listed (examples: *cat, cut, coat, cost*). Give the class one minute for the activity. Afterwards, have the students share their words as you write them on the board. Repeat the activity with a different pair of consonants.

TRICKY TONGUE TWISTERS

This activity lets students have fun with beginning consonant sounds. Write the following tongue twister on the board:

Sue saw seven seals swimming.

Call on a student to underline the beginning consonant of each word. Then have the class try saying the sentence three times quickly. Brainstorm other tongue twisters with the students, and write their suggestions on the board. Invite student volunteers to try saying the tongue twisters three times.

Next, divide the class into small groups. Challenge the groups to write tongue twisters for each consonant. (For *x*, you may want to let the students use words that have the letter in the final position.) Later, let the students of each group challenge the rest of the class to say their tongue twisters.

WHAT'S IN THE MIDDLE?

Check your students' discrimination of medial consonants by first writing the following list on the board:

ba___er   ti___er   ba___y

den___ist   bo___er   si___ent

Next, say the following words one at a time: *baker, tiger, baby, dentist, boxer, silent.* Each time, have a student fill in the missing consonant on the board. When all the words have been completed, tell the students to say the words aloud with you, and have them emphasize the sound of the medial consonant. For a follow-up activity, give a copy of page 6 to each student.

Off to School

Help the children get to the school. Name the pictures on the path. For each name, write the consonant that makes the beginning sound.

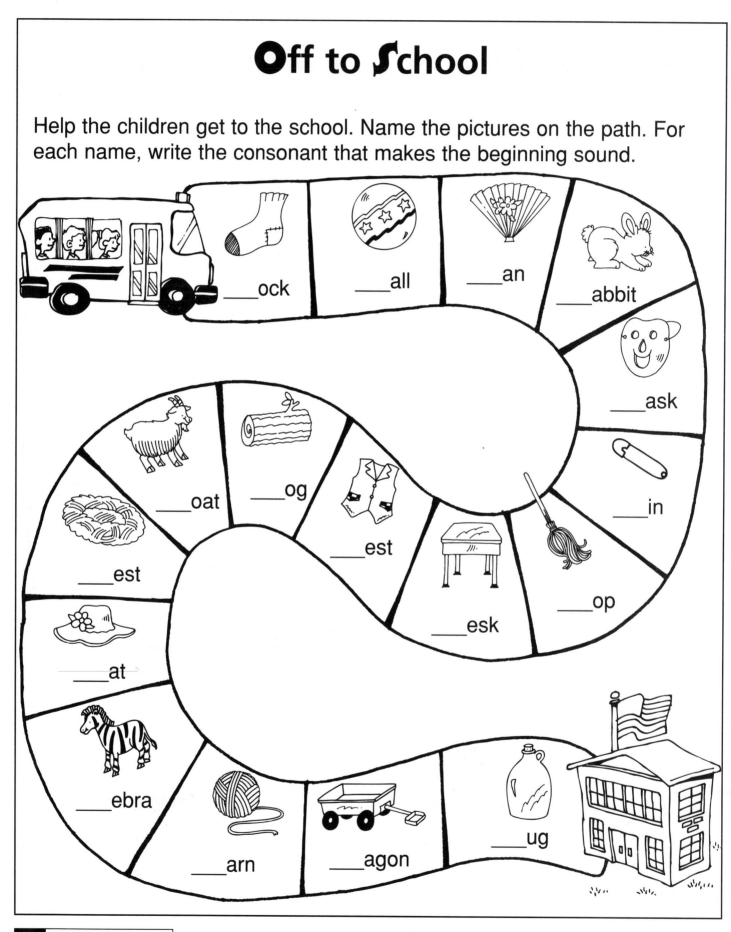

___ock

___all

___an

___abbit

___ask

___in

___op

___esk

___est

___est

___oat

___og

___at

___ebra

___arn

___agon

___ug

Set Sail With Consonants

Say the name of each picture on the sail. Write the consonant that makes the ending sound.

we___   be___   dru___   ca___

ba___   ne___   su___   pai___

lea___   fo___   bu___   ha___

ba___   to___   si___   wi___

Name _____

Around the Home

Write the missing
consonants.

___o___   ___a___   ___u__   ___e___

___oa___   ___o___   ___e__   ___u___

___a__   ___oo___   ___a___   ___oo___

___i___   ___ai___   ___u__   ___o___

FS123308 Phonics Made Simple—Grade 2 ■ © Frank Schaffer Publications, Inc.

A Web of Words

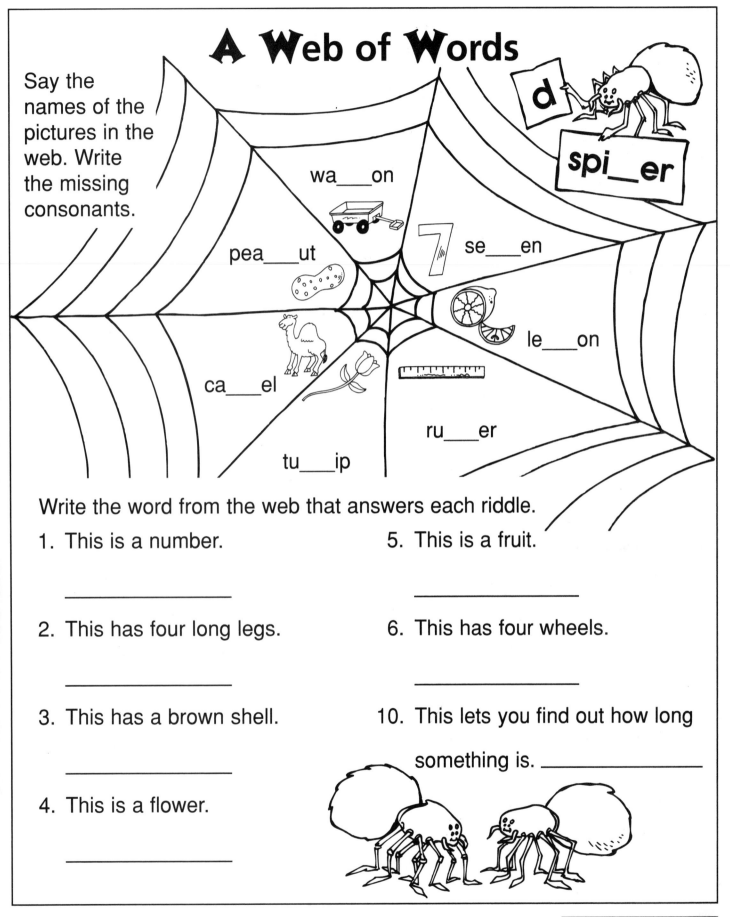

Say the names of the pictures in the web. Write the missing consonants.

d
spi__er

wa____on

pea____ut

7   se____en

le____on

ca____el

ru____er

tu____ip

Write the word from the web that answers each riddle.

1. This is a number.

_____

2. This has four long legs.

_____

3. This has a brown shell.

_____

4. This is a flower.

_____

5. This is a fruit.

_____

6. This has four wheels.

_____

10. This lets you find out how long

something is. _____

Short Vowels

Learning to hear, read, and write vowel sounds can be challenging for children. Since written English is not based on a purely phonetic system (the sound of long *a*, for example, can be written as *ai*, *ay*, or *ei*), a child can still apply the rules of phonics and misread or misspell a word. Since short vowels are more consistent in their spelling than long vowels, they are usually introduced before the other vowel sounds. Students in the second grade are already familiar with short vowels. A review of short vowels, however, will reinforce phonics skills and prepare students for more difficult concepts.

CONCEPTS

The ideas and activities presented in this section will help children develop the following skills:

- identifying short vowel sounds
- distinguishing words that contain short vowels
- reading and writing words with short vowels
- using context clues to choose the appropriate short vowel word

WHAT'S THE VOWEL?

Class Activity

Check your students' auditory discrimination of short vowels with this easy activity. Give each student five slips of paper, and instruct the children to write a vowel on each one. Then say a word, and have students hold up the paper that shows the vowel they hear. For example, if you say the word *hot*, the students should hold up the paper displaying *o*. Repeat the procedure several times, and include all five vowels in the activity.

PICK OUT THE WORDS

Class Activity

To prepare for this activity, write five sentences that have one or more words containing the short vowel your class is studying. For example, to review short *i* words, write a sentence such as *The pig is digging in his pen.*

Say the sentences one at a time to the class. Each time, have a student state the words containing the particular vowel sound. For an extra challenge, ask the class to spell the words as well.

Game

Word Relay

Make a set of cards with words containing short vowels. There should be at least as many words as you have students, and there should be the same number of words per vowel. Place the cards in a paper bag.

Divide the class into five teams and assign a different vowel to each one. Next, have one student at a time draw a card from the bag, read the word, and name the short vowel. The team assigned that vowel keeps the card. The first team to collect all the words available wins.

FS123308 Phonics Made Simple—Grade 2 ■ © Frank Schaffer Publications, Inc.

FLIP BOOKS

Visual Aid

Flip books provide a concrete way for students to see how word families are formed. To make a book, cut a 2" x 4" piece of tagboard. Then cut five or six 2" squares from lightweight paper. Attach the squares to the tagboard by stapling the pieces together along the short side. Next, write on the tagboard a short vowel word ending, such as *ack* or *and*. On the squares, write consonants that can be added to the word ending to create a word. For example, the letters *b, p, r, s,* and *t* can be blended with *ack*.

Make several sets of flip books that reinforce short vowel sounds. (These books are ideal for use with other kinds of word families as well, such as those involving long vowels or *r*-controlled vowels.) Leave the books at a center, and have students use them for a variety of activities. Here are some ideas:

- Write a sentence with each of the words.

- Write a story using as many of the words as possible.

- Make a word search puzzle with the words.

WORD WHEELS

Visual Aid

Word wheels help give students practice in reading and spelling words with short vowels. To make a word wheel, cut two identical circles from tagboard. Make the circles at least five inches in diameter. Cut out a "hole" about 1½" long and 1" wide from the edge of one circle. (The hole should not be too close to the circle's center.) Place the cut circle on top of the other one and attach the two in the center with a brad fastener.

Write a consonant on the top circle, near the front of the hole. Write a word ending on the bottom circle so that the letters form a word. Turn the bottom circle so that you have space to write another word ending. Continue writing word endings until you have at least five.

Store the word wheels in a box, and have each student select one as part of a reading or language arts activity. Students can read the words on their wheels and write sentences with them. Or, they can work with partners and choose two wheels instead; each child holds up a wheel, reads a word aloud, and asks his or her partner to spell it.

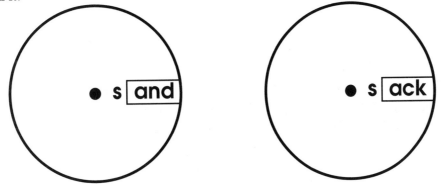

WORD CHALLENGE

Here's a fun way for students to practice writing short vowel words. Cut out 15 or more squares of construction paper. Write a letter on each square, making sure to include all five vowels. Then place the letters in a self-sealing plastic bag. Make several identical sets of letters.

Next, divide the class into small groups, and give each group a bag of letters. Challenge the students to use the letters to make as many short vowel words as they can. Have the groups list their words on a sheet of chart paper. Afterwards, let the groups share their lists with one another.

SHAPE PATTERNS ACTIVITIES

The shapes on page 10 can be used for a variety of activities reinforcing short vowels. Each shape corresponds to a short vowel—apple/short *a*; bell/short *e*; fish/short *i*; log/short *o*; duck/short *u*.

Scrambled Fun — Reproduce several copies of the patterns, and cut out each shape. Write scrambled words on the shapes, and display them where the class can see them easily. Challenge the students to unscramble the words. Here are some display ideas:

- Write scrambled short *a* words on the apples, and tape the apples to a paper apple tree.

- Write scrambled short *e* words on the bells, and tape the bells to lengths of yarn. Hang them against a wall or from a window.

- Write scrambled short *i* words on the fish, and tape the fish to butcher paper that has been cut into a large fishbowl.

- Write scrambled short *o* words on the logs, and display the logs on a bulletin board that has a border of paper leaves.

- Write scrambled short *u* words on the ducks, and pin them to a bulletin board that has been covered with blue paper.

A Path of Words — Cut out 10 or more shapes. Write a short vowel word on each shape. Make a path by taping the shapes along a wall. At the end of the path, leave a box of treats (such as sugar free gum or stickers). Ask the students to read all the words on the path, and then reward them with the treats.

Short Vowels Hunt — Reproduce a copy of page 10 for each child. Then have the students look through their readers or library books for short vowel words, and have them write the words on the appropriate shapes. Challenge the students to find at least three examples of each short vowel.

Shape Patterns

short a

short i

short e

short u

short o

SPELLING SENTENCES

Give students practice writing short vowel words by occasionally dictating five simple sentences that the class has not seen before. (Examples: *A cat sat on Pat's lap. Ten men slept in tents.*) By using sentences that the children have not practiced, you will be able to see how well they can apply phonetic rules of spelling. This activity also lets you see if students can apply rules of capitalization and punctuation.

SHORT VOWEL CLUES

Write words with short vowels on slips of paper, and place the papers facedown in a box. Call on a student to pick up a paper and read the word silently. Then have the child state one or more clues about the word while the rest of the class guesses. For example, if the word is *duck*, then a clue might be *This bird is a good swimmer*. The student who guesses the word also spells it aloud. That child then becomes the next person to choose a word and give clues about it.

Game

Draw and **S**pell

Let your students play this drawing game to reinforce their ability to spell short vowel words. First, write words with short vowels on index cards. The words should be ones that can be illustrated easily, such as *lamp* or *ring*. Place the cards in a paper bag. Next, divide the class into two teams. Then ask one member of a team to select a card from the bag. That child reads the word silently and at your signal illustrates it on the board. His or her team gets 30 seconds to guess the word. If the members of the team guess the word correctly, they get one point. If a child on the team is then able to spell the word, his or her team gets another point. Repeat the procedure by calling a member from the other team and letting that team guess the next word. Continue playing the game until all the students have had a chance to draw on the board.

Name _____

Short a Words

Circle the word for each picture. Write it on the line.

had / hat	bag / ban	rat / ram
_____	_____	_____
ham / hag	tan / tack	cab / cat
_____	_____	_____
jam / jab	fan / fat	sad / sack
_____	_____	_____
van / vat	mad / mat	bat / back
_____	_____	_____
has / hand	pat / pan	last / lamp
_____	_____	_____

FS123308 Phonics Made Simple—Grade 2 ▪ © Frank Schaffer Publications, Inc.

Short e Words

Circle the word for each picture. Write it on the line.

bet / bed	hen / hem	net / neck
pen / pet	jet / jest	tell / ten
test / tent	web / went	met / men
net / nest	bell / bent	let / leg
belt / bent	dent / desk	vest / vent

FS123308 Phonics Made Simple—Grade 2 ■ © Frank Schaffer Publications, Inc.

Short i Words

Circle the word for each picture. Write it on the line.

pig / pit	
fit / fish	
ring / rink	
six / sit	
win / wig	
pin / pill	
miss / mitt	
sing / sink	
bib / bit	
lit / lid	
milk / mink	
gill / gift	
did / dish	
king / kiss	
hid / hill	

15

Short o Words

Circle the word for each picture. Write it on the line.

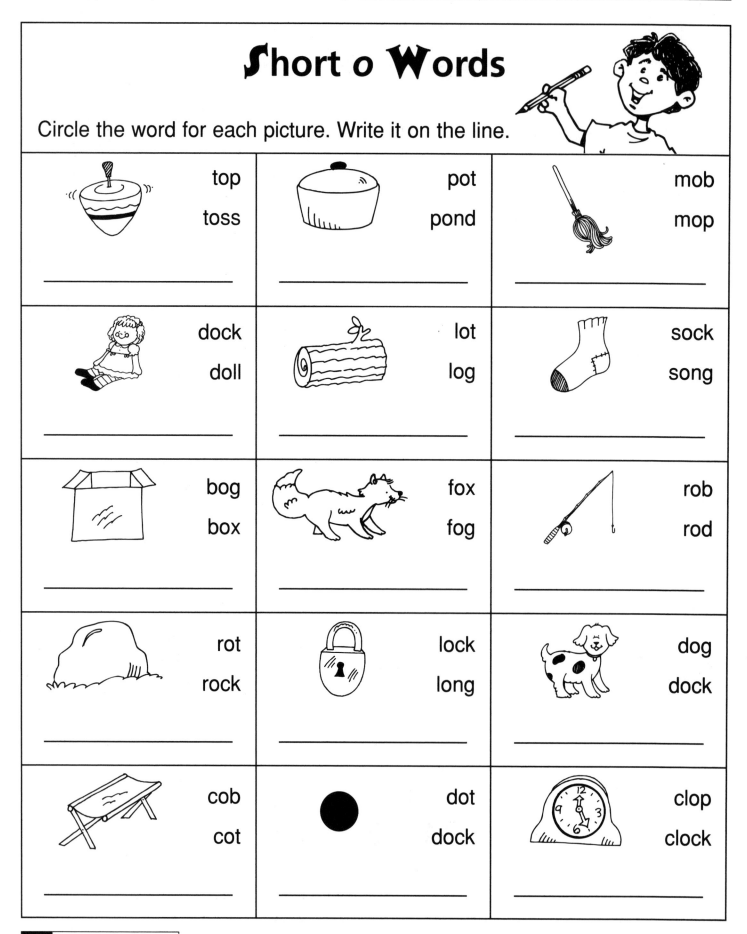

top / toss	pot / pond	mob / mop
dock / doll	lot / log	sock / song
bog / box	fox / fog	rob / rod
rot / rock	lock / long	dog / dock
cob / cot	dot / dock	clop / clock

FS123308 Phonics Made Simple—Grade 2 ■ © Frank Schaffer Publications, Inc.

Short u Words

Circle the word for each picture. Write it on the line.

cup / cut	sun / sum	hum / hut
but / bug	pup / pump	dug / duck
nun / nut	jug / just	gum / gull
rub / rug	sun / sub	run / rut
tub / tuck	but / bus	cut / cuff

Picnic Time

Help the ants get to the picnic basket. Label the pictures on the path.
Write **a**, **e**, **i**, **o**, or **u** on the lines.

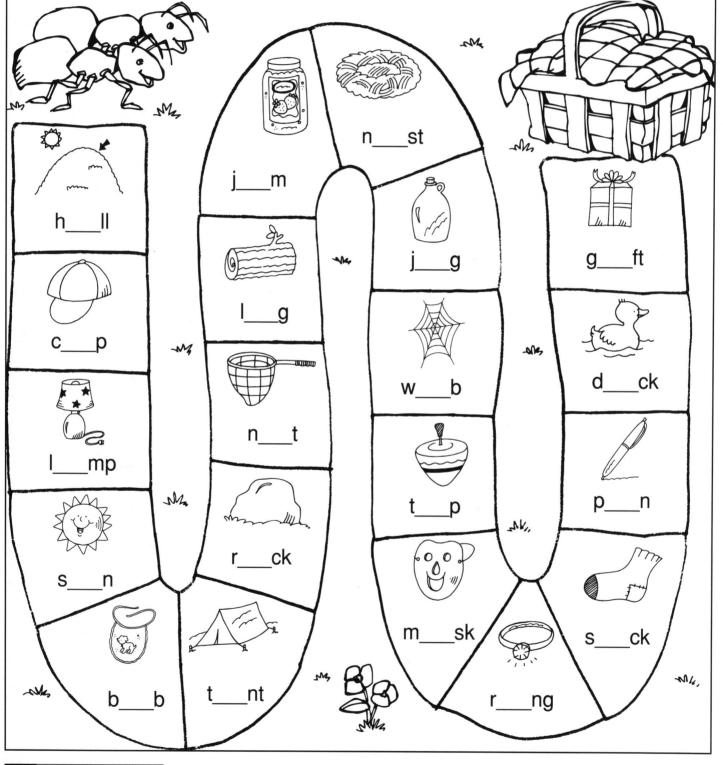

h___ll

c___p

l___mp

s___n

b___b

t___nt

j___m

l___g

n___t

r___ck

n___st

j___g

w___b

t___p

m___sk

r___ng

g___ft

d___ck

p___n

s___ck

FS123308 Phonics Made Simple—Grade 2 ▪ © Frank Schaffer Publications, Inc.

Long Vowels

Long vowels can be confusing for children because they are written in so many ways. A child who writes *rane* for *rain*, for example, demonstrates an ability to apply phonics rules; the misspelling occurs because he or she has chosen a "wrong," though legitimate, way to note the long *a* sound. In addition, there are many exceptions to a spelling rule. *Bike* and *give* have a similar spelling pattern (consonant-vowel-consonant-silent *e*), but the *i* is a long vowel in *bike* and a short vowel in *give*. Continued exposure to written language helps children remember which words are spelled with which rules and which are exceptions. The more children read and write, the more they learn about how English works, and the more they are able to deal with its inconsistencies.

CONCEPTS

The ideas and activities presented in this section will help children develop the following skills:

- *identifying long vowel sounds*
- *distinguishing words that contain long vowels*
- *reading and writing words with long vowels and silent e*
- *reading and writing words with vowel digraphs*
- *distinguishing between short vowels and long vowels*

EYE-CATCHING CHARTS

Class Activity

Introduce long vowel sounds one at a time, beginning with words that have similar spelling patterns, such as long *a* words containing silent *e*. (Ideas for teaching the various long vowel patterns begin on page 21.) Later, have students make charts displaying the various spelling patterns. Here are some ideas:

<u>Long a, silent e</u> – Have each child write a long *a* word on a paper oval. Tape all the ovals together to make one long snake.

<u>Long i, silent e</u> – Have groups of students write long *i* words on diamond-shaped paper. Then have students decorate the papers to make kites.

<u>Long o, silent e</u> – Have students write long *o* words on paper bones. Glue the bones to a chart on which you've drawn a dog. Label the chart *Bone Up on Long o Words*!

<u>Long u, silent e</u> – On chart paper, draw a mule carrying a large pack. Have the class help you write long *u* words on the pack.

<u>Long a (ai, ay)</u> – Have the class write *ai/ay* words on paper raindrops. Glue them onto a chart labeled *Rainy Day Words*.

<u>Long e (ee, ea)</u> – Have the class write *ee/ea* words on paper leaves, and glue them onto a paper tree trunk.

<u>Long o (oa)</u> – Have the class write *oa* words on paper boats. Display the boats on blue butcher paper.

VOWEL COLLECTION

Do this review activity after your students have been introduced to both short and long vowels. Give each student a 12" x 18" sheet of construction paper, and instruct the class to fold the papers in half. Have students label one-half of their papers *Short Vowels* and the other half *Long Vowels*. Then let the children look through magazines and newspapers for examples of words containing short and long vowels. Instruct students to cut out the words and glue them on the appropriate half of their papers. Have students also use highlighter pens to indicate the short or long vowels. (If a word has both a long and short vowel, such as *cupcake*, have the student choose which side of the paper he or she wants to include it on. If a word includes a vowel with a variant sound, such as *playground*, have the student only highlight the vowel that is short or long.)

SPELLING TIC-TAC-TOE

Game

Reinforce the spelling patterns of long vowel words with this game. Draw a 4 x 4 grid on the board. Then divide the class into two teams. Designate the first team as *X* and the second one as *O*. Ask the first team to spell a long vowel word. If a member spells the word correctly, have the child mark an *X* on the grid. Then ask the second team to spell a word, and have the child who answers correctly mark an *O* on the grid. (If a word is spelled incorrectly, simply ask the class for the correct spelling, but do not let students mark the grid.) Continue the procedure until all the spaces on the grid have been filled. Then add up the scores for the teams:

3 in a row — 1 point
4 in a row — 2 points

O	O	O	O
O	X	O	X
O	O	X	X
X	X	X	X

Team X – 5 points
Team O – 3 points

Variation: Use a 5 x 5 grid, and include a scoring of 5 in a row for 3 points.

Switch!

Here's a fun activity that gives your class practice distinguishing vowel sounds. Tell students to listen as you state some words. Tell them that they are to switch seats whenever they hear a word with, for example, the long *a* sound. Then begin saying a variety of words, including words with short vowels and long vowels (examples: *bat, pen, bike, rain*). As soon as students hear a word with long *a*, they are to quickly get out of their seats and sit elsewhere. The children sit in those seats until they hear another word with long *a*, at which point they move to other seats. Repeat the activity several times.

Long Vowels, Silent e

INTRODUCING LONG "A," SILENT "E"   Class Activity

Write these words on the board: *at, cap, tap, pan,* and *mad.* Have the students read the words aloud, and note the short vowel sound in each one. Next, add *e* to the end of *at,* and read the word to the class. Tell the class that the sound of the *a* in *ate* is called *long a.* Then call on student volunteers to add *e* to the other words, and have the class read the new words.

For a follow-up activity, hold up flashcards of short *a* and long *a* words. Have students read the words aloud as you display them one at a time. Then hold up the cards again, but this time have the students sit whenever they see a short *a* word and stand whenever they see a long *a* word.

INTRODUCING LONG "I," SILENT "E"   Class Activity

Write the following words on the board: *fin, hid, pin, rip,* and *bit.* Ask the students to read the words aloud, and have them notice the short *i* in each word. Next, add *e* to the end of *fin,* and read the word to the class. Have the students notice how the vowel sound changed. Tell the class that when the *i* "says its name," it is called a long *i.* Guide the students into seeing that the *e* at the end is silent, but that it changes the *i* to a long vowel. Add *e* to the remaining words, and have the class read the words aloud.

To reinforce the recognition of long *i* words, write short *i* and long *i* words on flashcards. Line up several of the cards against the chalkboard ledge. Then have one student at a time read the words in a row. Every so often, replace the words on the ledge with the other cards.

hid   ripe   line

INTRODUCING LONG "O," SILENT "E"   Class Activity

bone

Write the following words on the board: *hop, not, rod, rob,* and *mop.* Have the class read the words aloud and notice the short *o* in each word. Next, add *e* to the end of *hop,* and ask a student to read the word. Guide the class into seeing that the *e* changes the *o* to a long vowel. Add *e* to the remaining words, and have the students read the words aloud. Then give your class spelling practice by calling on two or three students at a time to go to the board and write long *o* words such as the following: *bone, cone, hole, home, hose, joke, nose, pole, rose, vote.*

INTRODUCING LONG "U," SILENT "E"

Write the following words on the board: *cub, cut,* and *tub.* Ask the students to read the words aloud, and have them notice the short *u* in each word. Next, add *e* to the end of each word, and have the students read the words. Let them see that the *e* changes the *u* to a long vowel.

For follow-up, write a variety of short *u* and long *u* words on the board. (Long *u* words can include *use, fuse, mule, rule,* and *tune.*) Ask one student at a time to read the words; instruct the children to circle the word if it has a short *u* and to underline it if it has a long *u.*

cube
cute
tube

CATERPILLAR PAIRS

Use the patterns on page 23 to make a chart reviewing words with long vowels and silent *e.* First, brainstorm with the class a list of short vowel words that can be made into long vowel words by adding *e* at the end (examples: *can, cap, fat, hat, mad, pan, rat, tap, bit, fin, hid, rip, pin, spin, cod, hop, mop, not, rob, rod, cub, cut, tub, us*). Write the words on the board.

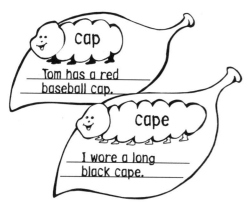

cap
Tom has a red baseball cap.

cape
I wore a long black cape.

Next, give a copy of the patterns to each student. Tell the class to write a short vowel word on the short caterpillar and a corresponding long vowel word with silent *e* on the long caterpillar. (The students may use the suggestions on the board or come up with words of their own.) Instruct the children to also write a sentence with their words on the leaves. Afterwards, have the students color their caterpillars and cut them out. Pin the caterpillars on a bulletin board for a colorful display.

Game

Long Vowels Scavenger Hunt

Reproduce a copy of page 24 for each student. Have the class read the list on the page, and have students underline those words that have a long vowel sound. Then let the students take the papers home to search for the items on the list. Remind the children to check off each item they find and to record how many they found at the bottom of the page. Afterwards, have the children return their papers to school so that they can compare one another's results.

FS123308 Phonics Made Simple—Grade 2 ■ © Frank Schaffer Publications, Inc.

Caterpillar Pairs

Think of a short vowel word that can be made into a long vowel word by adding an *e* to the end. Write the short vowel word on the short caterpillar. Write the long vowel word on the long caterpillar. Then think of a sentence for each of the words. Write the sentences on the leaves.

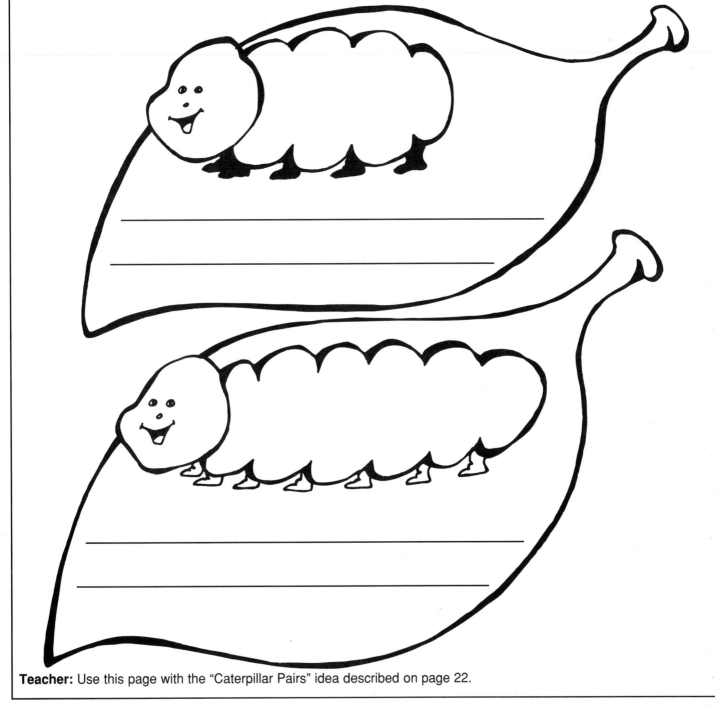

Teacher: Use this page with the "Caterpillar Pairs" idea described on page 22.

Long Vowels Scavenger Hunt

Read the list below. Underline the words that have long vowels. Then look for each of the items in your home. Check off the ones you find.

_____ a rake	_____ a red rose	_____ a grape
_____ a spade	_____ a tube	_____ a joke book
_____ ice cubes	_____ a flute	_____ a long rope
_____ a big plate	_____ a white stove	_____ some lace
_____ a small plate	_____ a garden hose	_____ a toy plane
_____ masking tape	_____ a wooden pole	_____ a tire
_____ a fun game	_____ five dimes	_____ a butter knife
_____ a cute toy	_____ a kite	_____ a phone
_____ an odd shape	_____ a candy cane	_____ a price tag

How many items did you find? _____

Teacher: Use this page with the "Long Vowels Scavenger Hunt" idea described on page 22.

 FS123308 Phonics Made Simple—Grade 2 ▪ © Frank Schaffer Publications, Inc.

Name _____

A Plane Ride

Use the words on the plane to complete the sentences.

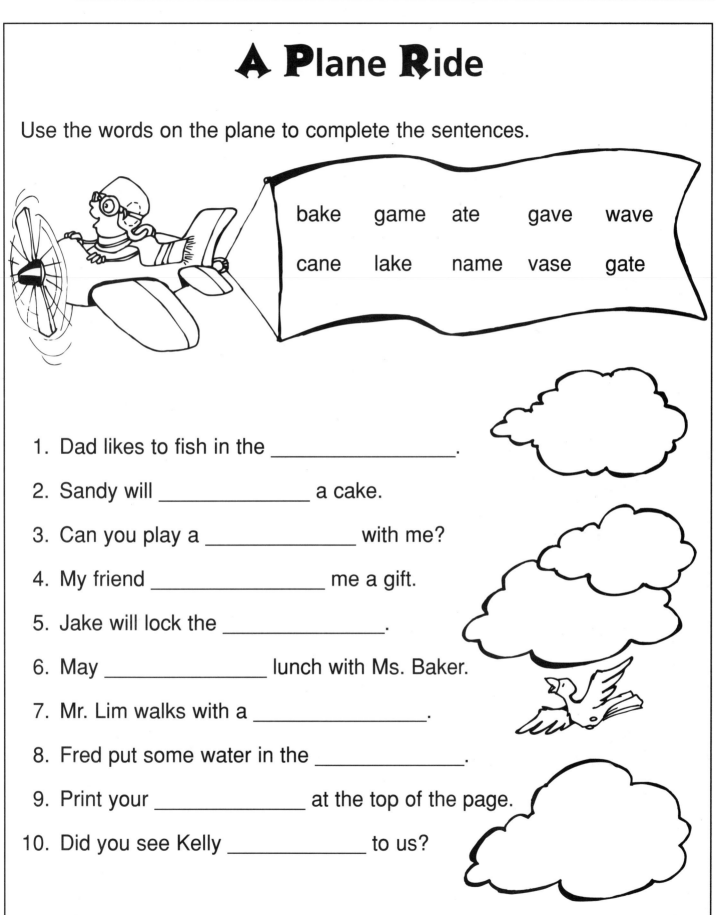

bake   game   ate   gave   wave

cane   lake   name   vase   gate

1. Dad likes to fish in the _____.

2. Sandy will _____ a cake.

3. Can you play a _____ with me?

4. My friend _____ me a gift.

5. Jake will lock the _____.

6. May _____ lunch with Ms. Baker.

7. Mr. Lim walks with a _____.

8. Fred put some water in the _____.

9. Print your _____ at the top of the page.

10. Did you see Kelly _____ to us?

A Busy Hive

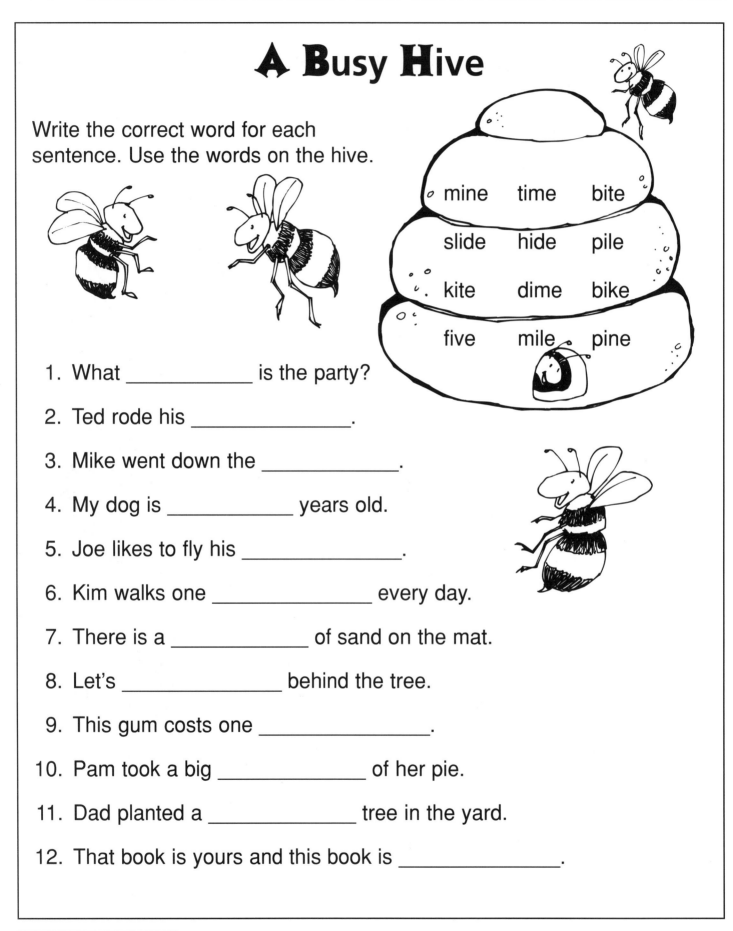

Write the correct word for each sentence. Use the words on the hive.

Words on the hive:
mine   time   bite
slide   hide   pile
kite   dime   bike
five   mile   pine

1. What _____ is the party?

2. Ted rode his _____.

3. Mike went down the _____.

4. My dog is _____ years old.

5. Joe likes to fly his _____.

6. Kim walks one _____ every day.

7. There is a _____ of sand on the mat.

8. Let's _____ behind the tree.

9. This gum costs one _____.

10. Pam took a big _____ of her pie.

11. Dad planted a _____ tree in the yard.

12. That book is yours and this book is _____.

   FS123308 Phonics Made Simple—Grade 2 ▪ © Frank Schaffer Publications, Inc.

Long o Roundup

Use the long *o* words inside the rope to complete each sentence.

home   pole   woke   hole   robe

hope   rose   hose   rode   note

1. The dog dug a _____ in the yard.

2. Mom put the _____ in a vase.

3. Joe wrote a _____ to his friend.

4. I _____ it will not rain today.

5. Emma _____ the bus to school.

6. We must get _____ before dinner.

7. Linda _____ up late this morning.

8. The king wore a long _____.

9. Cory put his fishing _____ in the car.

10. Mom used a _____ to water the garden.

Luke's List

Look at Luke's list. Use the words
to complete the sentences.

cube	tune
cute	mule
use	rule
tube	flute

1. Sue's puppy is _____.

2. You may _____ my ruler.

3. A _____ can carry a big pack.

4. Ben put an ice _____ in his glass.

5. Kris is learning to play the _____.

6. I forgot the _____ of that song.

7. What is inside the blue _____?

8. A king may _____ for many years.

Use four of the words from Luke's list to label the pictures.

9. _____ 10. _____ 11. _____ 12. _____

    FS123308 Phonics Made Simple—Grade 2 ■ © Frank Schaffer Publications, Inc.

A Long Hike

Help the children finish their hike. Label the pictures. Write **a**, **i**, **o**, or **u** on the lines.

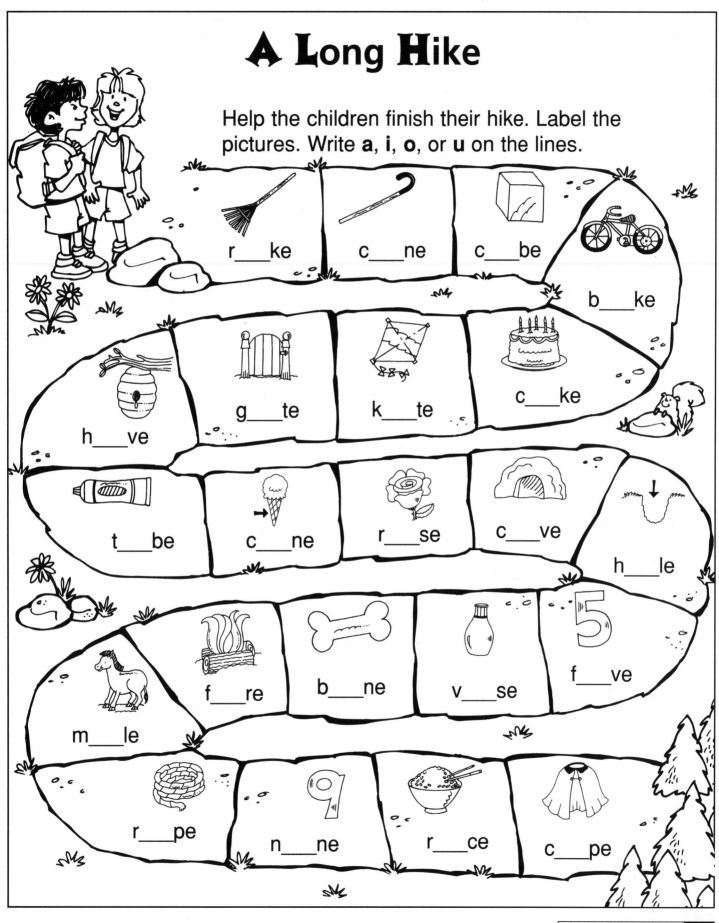

r___ke

c___ne

c___be

b___ke

h___ve

g___te

k___te

c___ke

t___be

c___ne

r___se

c___ve

h___le

m___le

f___re

b___ne

v___se

f___ve

r___pe

n___ne

r___ce

c___pe

A Fine Day

Circle the missing word for each sentence. Write it on the line.

	1. Jake rode his _____.	bite bone bike
	2. Meg fished in the _____.	like lake lane
	3. Carl helped _____ the yard.	rake ride rate
	4. Kate played a _____ on her flute.	time tube tune
	5. Jeff baked a _____.	cake code cave
	6. Gus planted a _____ bush.	rise rule rose
	7. Tara played with her _____ kitten.	cane cute cone

FS123308 Phonics Made Simple—Grade 2 ■ © Frank Schaffer Publications, Inc.

Vowel Digraphs

Digraphs are two letters that produce a single sound, such as *ph* in *phone* or *ea* in *head*. In this section, you'll find activities for teaching the long vowel digraphs *ai, ay, ee, ea* (as in *team*), and *oa*.

A PAIL OF OBJECTS

Class Activity

Place the following objects in a pail: a nail, some paint, mail (such as letters and flyers), a chain, and a braid (a length of braided yarn). Show the pail to the class and write *pail* on the board. Then take out the objects one at a time, and have the students name them. Write the words on the board. Have students notice that in each word the long *a* sound is produced by *ai*. Then dictate these words and call on student volunteers to write them on the board: *hail, jail, rail, sail, tail, bait, wait, pain, maid*.

For a follow-up activity, write the following sentences on the board:

A maid helps in the home.

All dogs have long tails.

Hail falls from the sky.

A snail has legs.

We sometimes paint at school.

You need bait to catch fish.

Have students point out the *ai* words. Then ask the class to read the sentences aloud and tell whether the statements are true or false.

A WORD TRAY

Class Activity

To prepare for this activity, write these words on flashcards: *bay, clay, crayon, day, gray, hay, jay, pay, play*. Lay the flashcards facedown on a tray.

Call on one student at a time to pick up a flashcard, read the word, and tape it to the board. After all the words are displayed, have the students point out that the long *a* sound in each word is produced by *ay*.

Next, ask the students to look at the flashcards to find the answers to these riddles:

Horses eat this. (hay)

This is a bird. (jay)

This is a body of water. (bay)

This is a color. (gray)

You do this at recess. (play)

This is made up of 24 hours. (day)

You can shape this into a ball. (clay)

You use this to color a picture. (crayon)

You do this when you buy something. (pay)

As the answers are found, have a child take the corresponding flashcard and put it back on the tray.

LONG "E" SHOPPING SPREE

Class Activity

Bring a large grocery bag to school. Tell the class that you went on a shopping spree and bought a lot of items. Then take out these foods (or pictures of food) from the bag: peas, beans, cream, peach, tea, beets, cheese, sunflower seeds, ground beef. After the bag has been emptied, have the class help you list the items on the board. Have the students notice that the long *e* sound can be produced by *ea* or *ee*. Tell the children that though they cannot rely on the sound of *ea* and *ee* to help them spell long *e* words correctly, they will become familiar with the words the more they read and write.

For a follow-up activity, have the children look through readers and library books to make a chart of *ea/ee* words. (See page 19 for chart ideas.) Then challenge the students to write one or more sentences using as many of the *ea/ee* words as they can.

LISTEN, READ, AND SPELL

Class Activity

Say these words to the class and have the students state the common sound in each: *boat, coat, goal, road, soap* (long *o*). Write the words on the board, and have the class notice that the long *o* sound is produced by *oa*. Then hold up flashcards of other *oa* words, and have the class read them aloud: *goat, load, oak, oat, loaf, soak, toad, toast*.

Reinforce the reading and spelling of *oa* words by calling on three or four students at a time to go to the board. Dictate an *oa* word, and have each student write it; the rest of the class can check the words to make sure they are correct.

Art Project

Silly Scenes

Divide the class into five groups, and assign each group one of these vowel digraphs: *ai, ay, ee, ea, oa*. Give each group a large sheet of drawing paper, and tell the students that they are to draw a silly scene illustrating as many words containing their vowel pair as they can. For example, a group assigned *ai* might show a quail with a long tail painting a picture; a train carrying a load of snails can be traveling along railroad tracks. After the pictures are finished, have each group display its drawing while the rest of the students look for the words that were illustrated.

A Rainy Day

Add **ai** to the words in the pail.

r_____n

sn_____l

t_____l

gr_____n

Add **ay** to the words on the haystack.

d_____

st_____

gr_____

pl_____

Use the words you made to complete the sentences.

1. The sky was _____.

2. It was a cold _____.

3. A _____ crawled along the gate.

4. The cow swished her _____.

5. The horse ate some _____.

6. The chicks tried to _____ tag.

7. Soon it started to _____ hard.

8. Farmer Ray had to _____ in the barn.

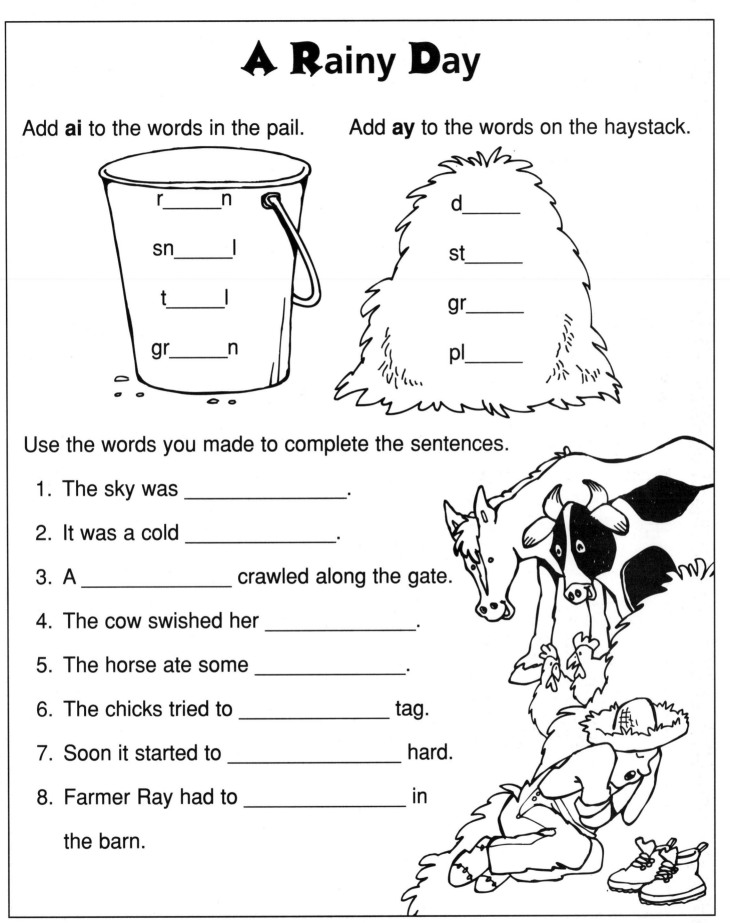

Read **C**arefully

Write the correct word for each sentence.

1. A _____ has wings.
   bee, fee

2. Lee will _____ me by the tree.
   meet, meek

3. It is time to _____ the dog.
   feet, feed

4. This pie is _____.
   see, sweet

5. Let's plant this _____.
   seek, seed

6. Zeke likes to _____ in a tent.
   sleep, steep

7. My dad is six _____ tall.
   feet, free

8. I _____ to get some books.
   weed, need

Leafy Words

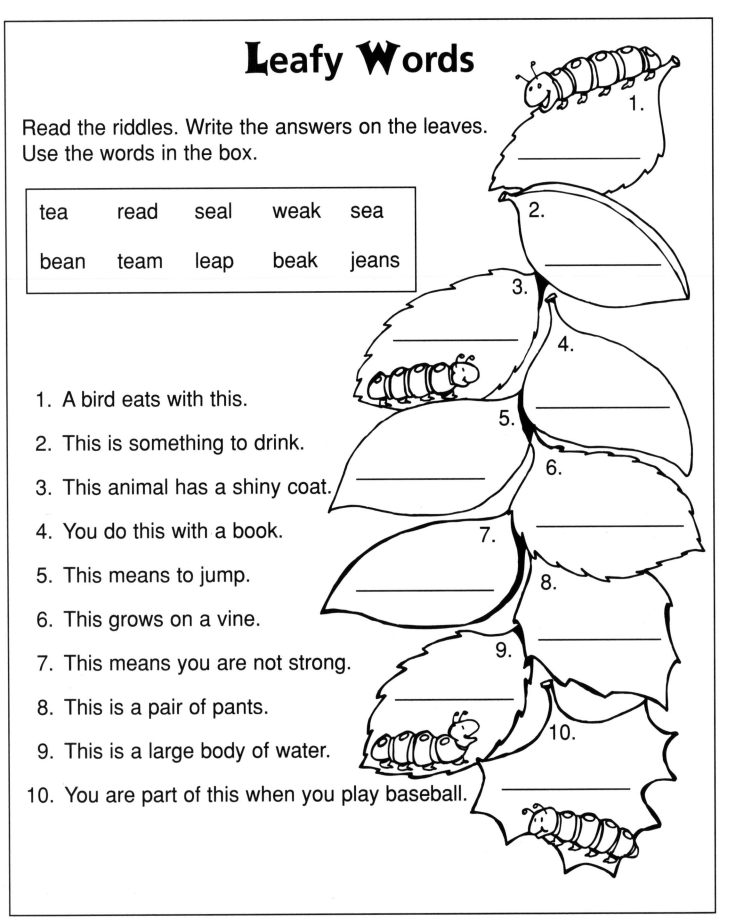

Read the riddles. Write the answers on the leaves.
Use the words in the box.

tea	read	seal	weak	sea
bean	team	leap	beak	jeans

1. A bird eats with this.

2. This is something to drink.

3. This animal has a shiny coat.

4. You do this with a book.

5. This means to jump.

6. This grows on a vine.

7. This means you are not strong.

8. This is a pair of pants.

9. This is a large body of water.

10. You are part of this when you play baseball.

1.

2.

3.

4.

5.

6.

7.

8.

9.

10.

Name _____

Drawing Fun

Underline the **oa** words below. Then finish the pictures to match the words.

a goat eating oats

a coat on the road

a toad with some toast

a big load of coal

a floating boat

soap on a toaster

Write the **oa** words you found.

_____ _____ _____

_____ _____ _____

_____ _____ _____

_____ _____ _____

FS123308 Phonics Made Simple—Grade 2 ■ © Frank Schaffer Publications, Inc.

Name _____

Toad's Riddles

Use the words in the box to answer Toad's riddles.

rain
soap
gray
feet
road
leaf
meat

1. You use this to clean. ▢◯▢▢

2. You need to cook this. ◯▢▢▢

3. You have two of these. ▢▢◯▢

4. This is a path. ◯▢▢▢

5. This falls from the sky. ▢▢▢◯

6. This is on a tree. ◯▢▢▢

7. This is a color. ◯▢▢▢

Find out what Toad is saying. Write the circled letters on the numbered lines.

C __ __ __ __ __ __ __ __ __ __ __ !
   1 6 1 4   2 3   7 4 3 3 5

Long Vowel Challenge

Circle the word for each picture. Write it on the line.

gate	hay	bee
goat	hail	bay
goal	heal	beat
bean	rope	hide
bay	robe	hive
bone	read	hope
sail	mate	cut
seal	moat	cube
seek	meat	cute
late	tea	bike
loaf	tame	bait
leaf	tail	beak
soap	rack	pan
sip	rake	pay
soak	road	pail

FS123308 Phonics Made Simple—Grade 2 ▪ © Frank Schaffer Publications, Inc.

Consonant Blends and Digraphs

Consonant blends are two or more consonants that are combined to produce a "blended" sound, such as the *bl* in *black* or the *st* in *stop*. Consonant digraphs, on the other hand, are two consonants that form one sound, such as *ch* or *sh*. By the time children are working with blends and digraphs in their phonics and spelling programs, they are already familiar with short vowel and long vowel word patterns. Second graders will easily discover that if they can read short and long vowel words such as *rag* and *bake*, they can apply similar phonetic rules to read words such as *flag* and *shake*.

CONCEPTS

The ideas and activities presented in this section will help children develop the following skills:

- *identifying consonant blends and digraphs*
- *distinguishing between two or more consonant blends*
- *distinguishing between two or more consonant digraphs*
- *reading and writing words with consonant blends and digraphs*

INTRODUCING BLENDS AND DIGRAPHS

Organization

Introduce blends and digraphs in phonetic groups. For example, present *l* blends first (*bl, cl,* and so on), and later move on to *r* blends and *s* blends. Similarly, present *sh* and *ch* words separately from *wh* and *th* words.

Some blends and digraphs can be found in the middle or at the end of words. For example, *stay, toaster,* and *list* contain the *st* blend. Present blends and digraphs in the initial position first; later, introduce words with the particular sound in the medial or final position. For example, teach the *sh* sound by presenting words such as *ship, shell,* and *shake.* Then have the students listen as you say words such as *wish, mushroom,* and *finish,* and ask them to identify the position of the *sh*.

Game

flag
crust
fresh
GLUE

Add It Up

In this word hunt activity, students earn points for the words they find. To begin, divide the class into small groups and give each group a large sheet of paper and some magazines. Instruct the groups to look through the magazines and cut out examples of words containing blends and/or digraphs. Have the students glue the words onto their papers. Tell them that they will score one point for every word found; a word with two blends and/or digraphs, however, is worth five points. Give the class about 20 minutes for the activity. Afterwards, let each group display its words while the class adds up the score.

Consonant Blends

BLENDING WITH WORD WHEELS

Class Activity

Make word wheels (see page 8) that give students practice reading words with blends. Make a word wheel for each of the various blends. For example, create a word wheel of *bl* words and another one of *br* words. Leave the wheels at a table for students to use independently. Students may read the words to a partner, give one another spelling dictation, or write sentences with the words. Let students who need extra phonics practice take one or more word wheels home to read with their parents.

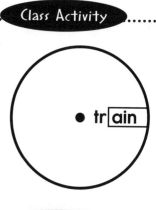

FLOWERY BLENDS

Class Activity

Divide the class into pairs, and assign each pair a blend. Next, have the students cut out a paper circle and write their blend on it. Then have the children cut out several paper petals and on them write words containing their blend. Have the children glue the pieces on construction paper to form a flower. Display the flowers on a bulletin board for a colorful display.

CLEVER CLUES

Class Activity

Challenge your class with this thinking game. First think of a word that contains a blend. Then write the word on the board, leaving out every other letter. Next, give a clue about the word, such as the following;

s__i__e — You can play on this in a park. (slide)

f__u__t — This is a type of food. (fruit)

b__a__k__t — This keeps you warm in bed.
        (blanket)

Let the child who guesses the word fill in the blanks on the board.

Art Project

A Blends Collage

Invite students to bring to school small disposable items, or pictures of items, that have names containing blends (examples: crayon, flower, flag, paper clip, plastic wrap, price tag, blades of grass). Have the students label their items and tape them to a large sheet of poster board. Title the display *A Blends Collage.*

FS123308 Phonics Made Simple—Grade 2 ■ © Frank Schaffer Publications, Inc.

A Tower of Blocks

Write the missing letters. Use the letters on the blocks.

1. Molly wore _____oves in the snow.

2. Clara will _____ant some bean seeds.

3. Glen has a _____ack kitten.

4. A _____ock helps us tell time.

5. Jay went down the hill on his _____ed.

6. Let's _____ay a game.

7. The man is waving a _____ag.

8. I am _____ad to see you.

9. Mom put the ham on a _____ate.

10. I go to _____eep at nine o' clock.

11. We went on a trip by _____ane.

12. Be careful not to _____ip on the ice.

Crossword Fun

Look at the picture clues to fill in the puzzle. Use the words in the box.

| tree | crab | fruit | dress | grass |
| drum | frog | prize | braid | truck |

Across

3.

5.

6.

8.

Down

1.

2.

7.

4.

9.

Space Friends

Write the correct word for each sentence.
Use the words on the spaceships.

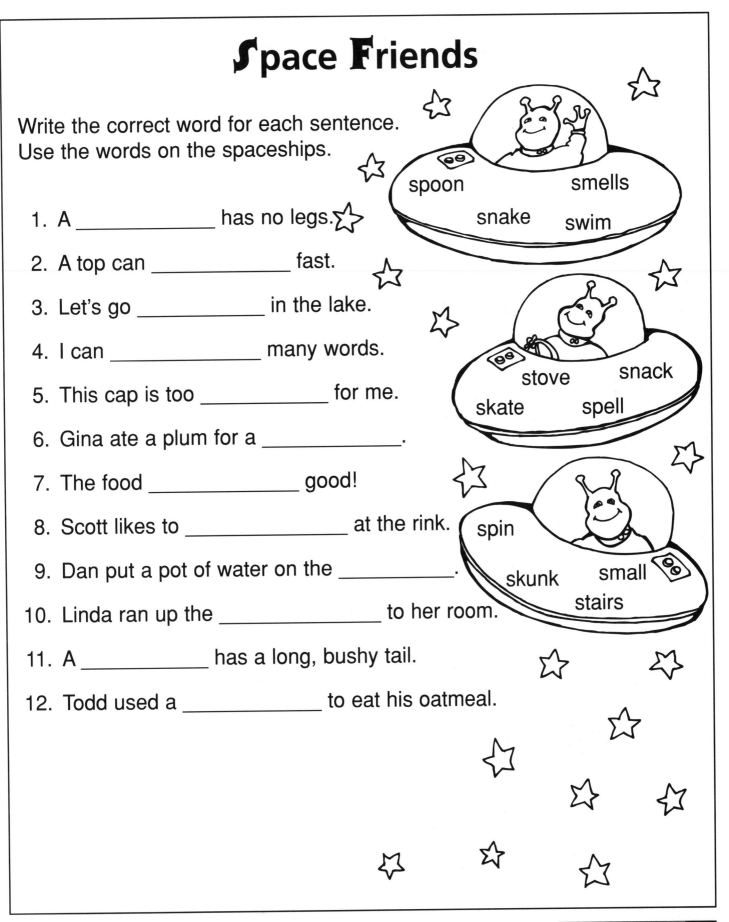

spoon   smells
snake   swim

stove   snack
skate   spell

spin
skunk   small
stairs

1. A _____ has no legs.

2. A top can _____ fast.

3. Let's go _____ in the lake.

4. I can _____ many words.

5. This cap is too _____ for me.

6. Gina ate a plum for a _____.

7. The food _____ good!

8. Scott likes to _____ at the rink.

9. Dan put a pot of water on the _____.

10. Linda ran up the _____ to her room.

11. A _____ has a long, bushy tail.

12. Todd used a _____ to eat his oatmeal.

Working With Blends

Circle the word for each picture. Write it on the line.

brick crack block	spin sled still	tree flee dream
glass grass cross	flag frog brag	grab class crab
skate slate stake	prize blast plate	slump snip stamp
globe gray float	plum truck drum	blimp brick trick
block clock crock	small slim snail	swing sting sling

  FS123308 Phonics Made Simple—Grade 2 ■ © Frank Schaffer Publications, Inc.

Consonant Digraphs

ON THE LOOKOUT FOR DIGRAPHS

Class Activity

Have your class keep a tally of words they find containing *ch, sh, th,* and *wh.* First, post four charts in the classroom, and label each one with one of the digraphs. During the week, let the students be on the lookout for words with digraphs. As students find words in their readers, textbooks, or other sources, let them write the words on the appropriate charts. Also have the children highlight the digraph in each word to show its position. At the end of the week, have the class count up the words to see which digraph appeared most often.

TONGUE TWISTER FUN

Class Activity

Tongue twisters with *ch, sh, th,* or *wh* can be especially hard to say. Let your students try the following: *Butch watched chubby chipmunks chew cheese. Sheryl shopped for shoes and brushes. Theo thinks thistles are thorny and thick. Warren wishes he were watching whales.*

Next, let your students work with a partner. Have each child write a tongue twister with words containing a particular digraph. Then have the students challenge their partners to say the tongue twisters quickly three times. Afterwards, let the children share their tongue twisters with the class.

MYSTERY WORD GAME

Class Activity

Here's a fun way to reinforce vocabulary skills. First, divide the class into Team A and Team B. Then have each team select a member to go in front of the board. Seat the two players so that they face the class. Then write on the board a "mystery word" containing *ch, sh, th,* or *wh.* The class will be able to see the word, but the two players will not. Then call on Team A to give a clue about the word. For example, if the word were *shell,* then a student might say *You can find this at the beach.* Team A's player then gets to guess the word. If the child guesses correctly, then Team A earns 10 points, and the round is finished. If the child guesses incorrectly, then Team B gives another clue, and Team B's player gets to guess the word for a score of 9 points. The teams take turns giving clues until the word is guessed; each time a clue is given, the score drops by one point. When the correct guess is made, two new players go to the front of the board for a new round.

Variation: Let the child who guesses the word also spell it for an extra point.

Shell

Chester's Challenge

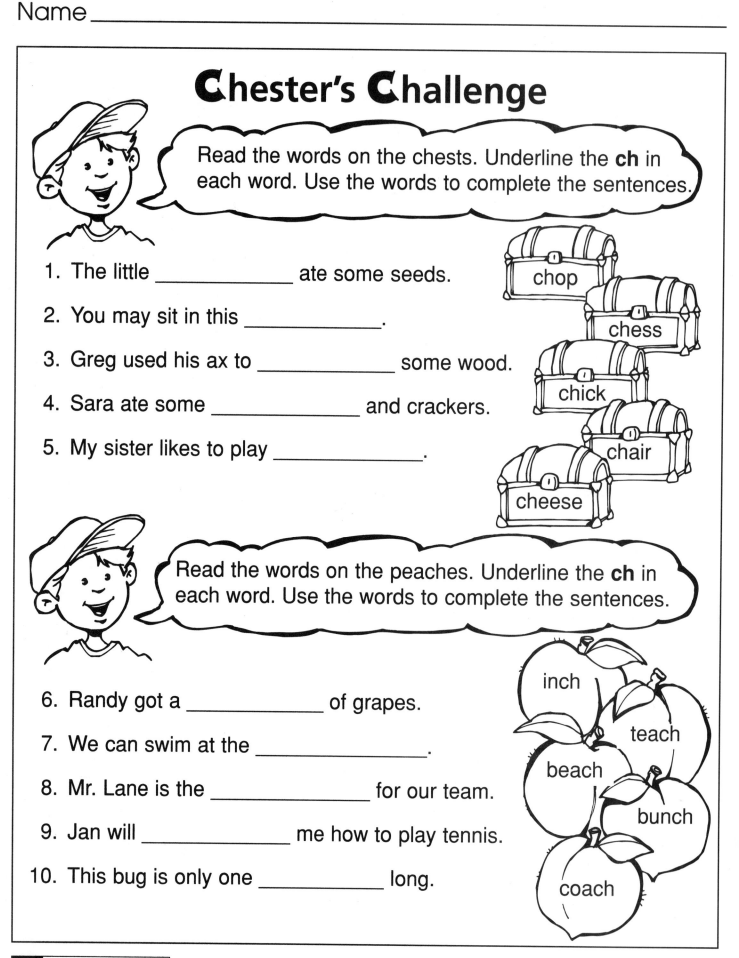

Read the words on the chests. Underline the **ch** in each word. Use the words to complete the sentences.

1. The little _____ ate some seeds.

2. You may sit in this _____.

3. Greg used his ax to _____ some wood.

4. Sara ate some _____ and crackers.

5. My sister likes to play _____.

chop

chess

chick

chair

cheese

Read the words on the peaches. Underline the **ch** in each word. Use the words to complete the sentences.

6. Randy got a _____ of grapes.

7. We can swim at the _____.

8. Mr. Lane is the _____ for our team.

9. Jan will _____ me how to play tennis.

10. This bug is only one _____ long.

inch

teach

beach

bunch

coach

FS123308 Phonics Made Simple—Grade 2 ■ © Frank Schaffer Publications, Inc.

Name _____

By the Shore

Write the missing word for each sentence. Use the words on the ship.

shop   ship   fish
shade   sheep   sash
shell   shelf   brush

1. Terry is taking a trip on a big _____.

2. We have to _____ for Ann's gift.

3. Please put the book back on the _____.

4. Many _____ live in the lake.

5. I _____ my teeth after I eat.

6. Let's stand in the _____ to stay cool.

7. This dress has a long _____.

8. A _____ was eating grass.

9. A snail has a _____ on its back.

Four words from the list are pictured above. Write them on the lines.

_____

Think About This!

Circle the missing word for each sentence. Write it on the line.

	1. Do you _____ it will rain?	thin thing think
	2. Thelma has _____ cats.	thrill three throat
	3. I take a _____ to stay clean.	with path bath
	4. A rose has _____ on its stem.	thorns thud theft
	5. This book is _____.	thick think thump
	6. A _____ has soft wings.	math with moth
	7. I will _____ Sam for the gift.	think thank thing

FS123308 Phonics Made Simple—Grade 2 ■ © Frank Schaffer Publications, Inc.

Which Word?

Write the correct word for each sentence.

1. A _____ can swim and dive.
   whale, whack

2. This muffin is made with _____.
   whiff, wheat

3. The _____ on the cart came off.
   while, wheel

4. My dog is black and _____.
   whip, white

5. Let's sit on this bench _____ we wait.
   while, whirl

6. A cat has _____ on its face.
   whisper, whiskers

7. The coach blew his _____.
   whistle, whether

8. Please tell me _____ the circus is coming.
   when, what

Find the Word

Circle the word for each picture. Write it on the line.

chip / ship / whip	thick / whiff / chick	cloth / clash / clutch
thorn / shin / chore	shell / while / whale	share / chair / whack
sheet / cheese / cheat	peach / path / plush	sheep / cheap / wheat
ditch / dish / dash	teach / three / teeth	shelf / shell / cheek
shell / wheel / chess	shed / chair / chest	wheat / sheet / white

FS123308 Phonics Made Simple—Grade 2 ■ © Frank Schaffer Publications, Inc.

R-Controlled Vowels

When the letter *r* follows a vowel, the sound of the vowel changes—in that respect, the sound of the vowel is "controlled" by the presence of *r*. For example, in the word *star*, the *a* is neither a short vowel nor a long vowel; instead the vowel takes on a whole new sound. As children work with words containing *r*-controlled vowels, they will see that *ar* and *or* are easily distinguishable; *er*, *ir*, and *ur*, on the other hand, produce the same sound. As in other cases in which the sound of a word gives few clues to its spelling, children will learn to spell words correctly through exposure and practice.

CONCEPTS

The ideas and activities presented in this section will help children develop the following skills:

- identifying words containing r-controlled vowels
- distinguishing between two or more r-controlled vowels
- reading and writing words with r-controlled vowels

WORDS IN A JAR
Class Activity

Write words containing *ar* (such as *car*, *arm*, *barn*, *star*, *part*, and *march*) on slips of paper, and place them in a jar. Show the jar to the class, and call on one student at a time to pull out a paper. Read the word and write it on the board. When all the slips have been drawn, have the students look at the list on the board. Help them see that the *ar* produces the common sound in each word.

For a follow-up activity, say the following riddles, and have students guess the *ar* word. Let the student who guesses correctly write the word on the board.

This shines in the sky. (star)

Children like to play here. (park)

It is the opposite of soft. (hard)

This is part of a tree. (bark)

This is a fish. (shark)

This is part of you. (arm)

This surrounds a house. (yard)

This is a musical instrument. (harp)

"AR" OR "OR"?
Class Activity

Say the following words to the class, and have students listen for the common sound: *fork*, *more*, *horn*, *pork*, *short*, and *store*. Write the words on the board, and have the students point out the *or* in each one. Then write other *or* words on the board, and have the class read them aloud (examples: *for*, *born*, *cork*, *horse*, *porch*, *snore*, *sport*, *storm*).

Next, play this simple game to check your students' auditory discrimination of *or*. Give each child two pieces of paper, and instruct the student to write *ar* on one paper and *or* on the other. Then say words containing either *ar* or *or*, and each time have students hold up the card displaying the corresponding letter pair.

A TRICKY TRIO

Say the following words to the class: *her, fern, dirt, stir, fur,* and *hurt.* Ask students what sound they hear in each word. Then write the words on the board. Have the class see that the letter pairs *er, ir,* and *ur* produce the same sound. Tell the students that as they practice reading and writing words containing these letter pairs, they will remember which letters are used with which words.

For follow-up, cut out stone-shaped pieces of paper. On each piece, write a word containing *er, ir,* or *ur.* Arrange the stones on a bulletin board to make a path. Pin a paper turtle at the beginning of the path and a second turtle at the end. Then ask the class to help the one turtle cross the path to meet its friend. Call on a student volunteer to read the first word on the path. When the word is read correctly, move the turtle to that stone. Continue asking students to read the words in order until the turtle has reached the end of the path.

girl burn her skirt curl clerk turn third

SUPER SENTENCES

Divide the class into five groups. Assign an *r*-controlled vowel to each group. Tell the students of each group to brainstorm words that have their assigned vowel. Let the students look in dictionaries to collect a variety of words. Then give each group a sheet of chart paper and have the students write "super" sentences with their words. Also have the groups underline the words containing the *r*-controlled vowels. Afterwards, let the groups share their sentences with the class.

A bird in a shirt chirped at a squirrel.

Game

ʃpell and ʃcore

Make flashcards with words containing *r*-controlled vowels. Label each card *1, 2,* or *3,* depending on the spelling level of the word. For example, rate *corn* and *fork* as *1* (words can be spelled phonetically), *horse* and *torch* as *2* (words have silent letters, blends, or digraphs), and *tornado* and *report* as *3* (words have two or more syllables). Place the cards in paper pockets marked *1, 2,* and *3.* Then divide the class into two teams. Ask a member from one team to select any card. When the card is chosen, read the word to the team, and have one of its members spell the word. If spelled correctly, the team scores the point marked on the card. If spelled incorrectly, then a student from either team can answer, but no points are given. Repeat the activity by asking the other team to select another card. Continue the game until each child has had a chance to spell. The team with the most points wins.

Farmer Martin

Write the correct word for each sentence.

1. Farmer Martin lives on a _____.
   far, farm

2. He works _____ all day long.
   hard, harm

3. Farmer Martin has animals in the _____.
   barb, barn

4. Farmer Martin loads his _____ with food.
   card, cart

5. He goes to the _____ to sell his food.
   mark, market

6. Farmer Martin has a _____ dog named Ruff.
   large, lark

7. Ruff likes to play in the _____.
   yard, yarn

8. Ruff sometimes likes to _____ at the chickens.
   bar, bark

Shopping Time

Read the story. Write the correct word for each sentence.

Lori went shopping _____ food.
for, form

She got some ears of _____. She
cork, corn

also got some _____ chops.
pork, port

Cory went to a _____, too.
store, stork

He got a pair of _____. Then he
shore, shorts

went to a _____ shop to get a soccer ball.
sport, spore

Norman shopped for party _____. He got
horns, horse

_____ of them! He got some
forth, forty

plastic _____, too.
for, forks

Ernie's Riddles

Write the answers to Ernie's riddles.
Use the words on his list.

1. This is a note for someone.

   _____

2. This is a color. _____

3. This can fly. _____

4. This is a leafy plant. _____

5. This has long sleeves. _____

6. A cat has this on its skin. _____

7. This worker helps you when you are ill or hurt. _____

8. Seeds need to grow in this. _____

9. You will find this worker in a store. _____

10. This lets you put a nail in wood. _____

fur	dirt
fern	clerk
nurse	purple
bird	letter
shirt	hammer

Don't Get Fooled!

Circle the word for each picture. Write it on the line.

stir star store _____	curt cord corn _____	carp cork curl _____
bark bird burn _____	her harm harp _____	dirt dark dart _____
north nurse nerve _____	car cord card _____	fur far fork _____
hard horn hurt _____	churn cork clerk _____	purse park perch _____
car cart core _____	fern fort farm _____	short shirt shark _____

FS123308 Phonics Made Simple—Grade 2 ▪ © Frank Schaffer Publications, Inc.

Sporty Sentences

Write the correct word for each sentence.

1. Karla plays tennis with _____ friend.
her, hurt

2. Pat can kick the soccer ball _____.
for, far

3. Kent wants to race _____.
core, cars

4. We played football at the _____.
park, pork

5. Matt likes riding his _____.
horn, horse

6. Joan finished _____ in the race.
third, thorn

7. It is Wendy's _____ to bat.
turn, torn

8. The runners were very _____.
thirty, thirsty

Special Vowels

Many vowel combinations in English produce more than one kind of sound. For example, *ow* makes a long *o* sound in words like *throw*, but it produces an entirely different sound in *howl*. The *ea* in *head* makes a short vowel sound, but it defies the phonetic rule that "when two vowels go walking, the first does the talking." These and other vowel combinations can be considered "special" in the sense that they do not fit typical spelling or sound patterns. Because of this, they pose an extra challenge for children learning to read, write, and spell words containing these vowel combinations.

CONCEPTS

The ideas and activities presented in this section will help children develop the following skills:

- identifying words containing special vowels (ow, oo, aw, au, ew, and others)

- distinguishing between two or more special vowels

- reading and writing words with special vowels

- using context to determine which sound a particular special vowel might produce

HELPFUL HINTS

Organization

Here are some hints for helping your students master special vowels:

▪ Present the special vowels one at a time. For example, introduce *ow* words with the long *o* sound *(snow)* first. When your class has become familiar with these *ow* words, then present *ow* words like *how*. In a later lesson, present *ou* words like *house*. (See suggestions for teaching *ow* and *ou* on page 59.)

▪ Have the students make colorful charts for each special vowel. Post the charts in the classroom as a reference for writing activities.

▪ Involve students in a variety of activities that let them practice reading and writing words containing special vowels. For example, have the class write sentences or stories using as many *oo* words as they can. Or, give them a list of words to look up in a dictionary; have the children write definitions for each word. Students can also make lists of rhyming words and write silly verses with the words. For example:

I saw a <u>mouse</u> build a <u>marshmallow</u> <u>house</u>.

Then he <u>took</u> a <u>spoon</u> and ate it at <u>noon</u>!

Have students underline all the words containing special vowels in their verses, even if the words are not the ones that rhyme.

FS123308 Phonics Made Simple—Grade 2 ▪ © Frank Schaffer Publications, Inc.

Ow (snow, how) and Ou (out)

LET IT SNOW!

Class Activity

Say the following words to the class, and have students point out the long *o* sound: *low, snow, grow, bowl, blow*. Write the words on the board, and have the children notice that *ow* makes the vowel sound. Next, write other *ow* words on the board, and have the class read them aloud (examples: *mow, row, glow, slow, crow, yellow, below, window, rainbow*).

Afterwards, have the class make a display by writing *ow* words on paper snowballs. Have a volunteer make a paper snowman and write *ow* on its body. Then glue the snowman and snowballs on blue paper labeled *Let It Snow!* For a follow-up activity, have students make up riddles about the *ow* words on the chart. (Example: You may see this in the sky after a rain.) Or, have them write a story using as many *ow* words as they can.

"OW" FLOWERS

Class Activity

Have students close their eyes as you say these words: *cow, how, down, gown,* and *howl*. Ask them what sound they hear in each word. Write the words on the board, and have the class see that the *ow* makes the sound common to each word. Write other *ow* words on the board, and have students read them aloud.

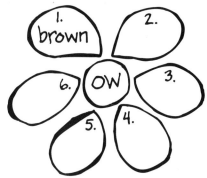

Next, give each student a sheet of paper on which a large flower has been drawn. The center of the flower has *ow* on it and there are six numbered petals around the flower. Then give the following riddles, and have students write the *ow* answers on the petals: 1. This is a color. (brown) 2. This person works at a circus. (clown) 3. A king wears this. (crown) 4. This is a long, fancy dress. (gown) 5. This is a large group of people. (crowd) 6. This is a light rain. (shower)

WHAT'S IN THE HOUSE?

Class Activity

Decorate a shoe box to make it look like a house. Next, write the following words on flashcards: *mouse, flour, couch, hound, blouse*. Add picture clues if you like, and then place the cards inside the box. Call on one student at a time to select a card from the house and read the word aloud. List the words on the board, and have the students see that *ou* makes the vowel sound in each word. (You may wish to point out that the *ou* sound in *house* is similar to the *ow* sound in *how*. Also point out the difference in meaning between *flour* and *flower*.)

For a follow-up activity, write other *ou* words on the board, but leave blanks for the vowels. Have students fill in the blanks with *ou* and read the words aloud (examples: *m___th, s___nd, ___t, cl___d*).

A Snowy Sign

Write the correct word for each sentence. Use the words on the sign.

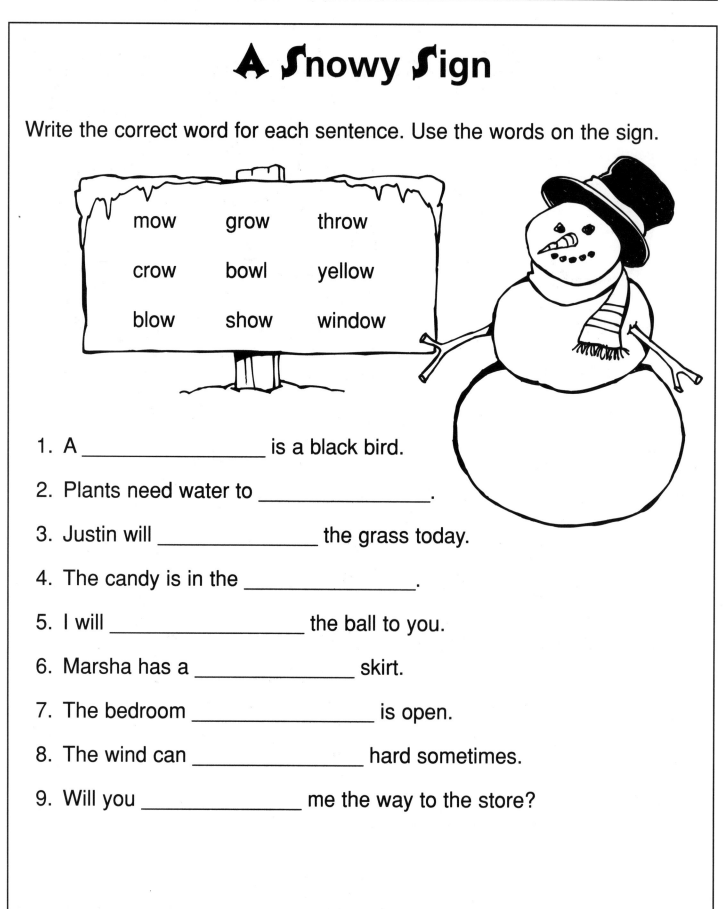

mow	grow	throw
crow	bowl	yellow
blow	show	window

1. A _____ is a black bird.

2. Plants need water to _____.

3. Justin will _____ the grass today.

4. The candy is in the _____.

5. I will _____ the ball to you.

6. Marsha has a _____ skirt.

7. The bedroom _____ is open.

8. The wind can _____ hard sometimes.

9. Will you _____ me the way to the store?

Clowning Around

Write the correct word for each sentence.
Use the words on the balloons.

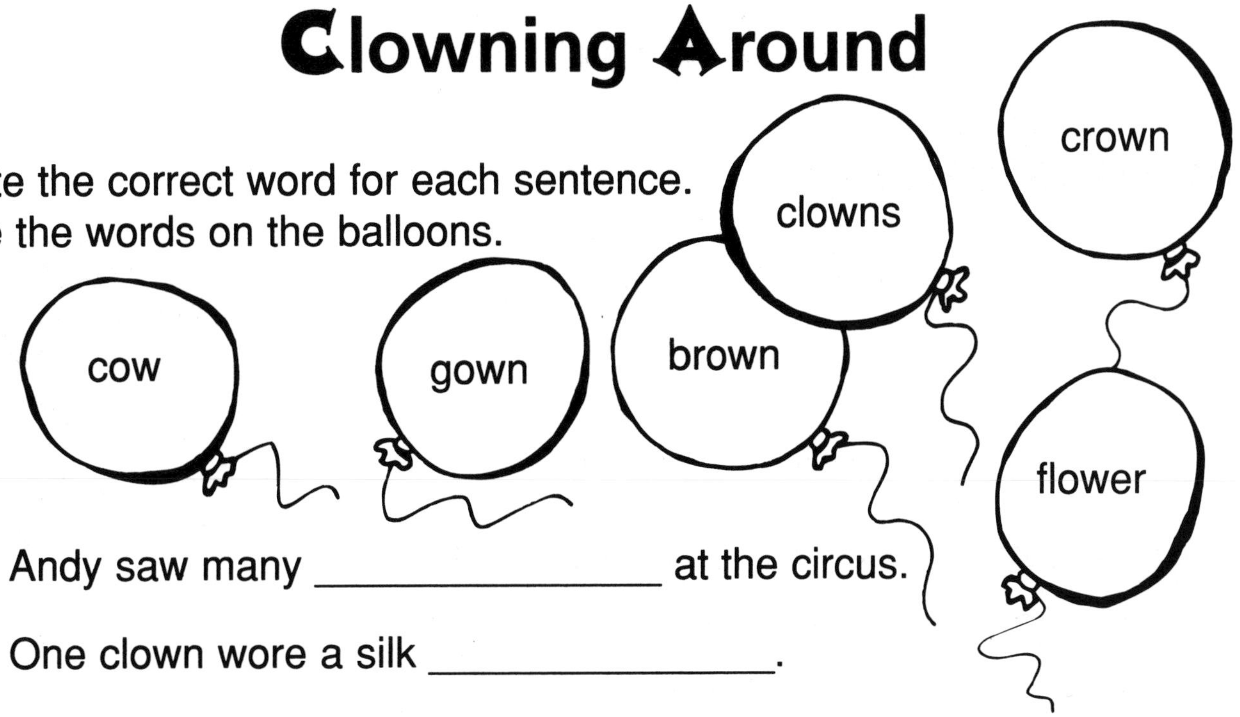

cow

gown

clowns

brown

crown

flower

1. Andy saw many _____ at the circus.

2. One clown wore a silk _____.

3. One clown was holding a _____ with a long stem.

4. One clown had a gold _____ on his head.

5. One clown wore a big _____ hat.

6. One clown walked out with his pet _____.

Draw one of the clowns that
Andy saw. Write a sentence
about your picture.

_____

_____

_____

_____

Two Sounds

Draw lines from the words to the pictures.

cow

bow

owl

crow

bowl

gown

crown

pillow

Write the words from the box in the correct column.

ow as in **snow**

_____

_____

_____

_____

ow as in **clown**

_____

_____

_____

_____

FS123308 Phonics Made Simple—Grade 2 ■ © Frank Schaffer Publications, Inc.

In the Clouds

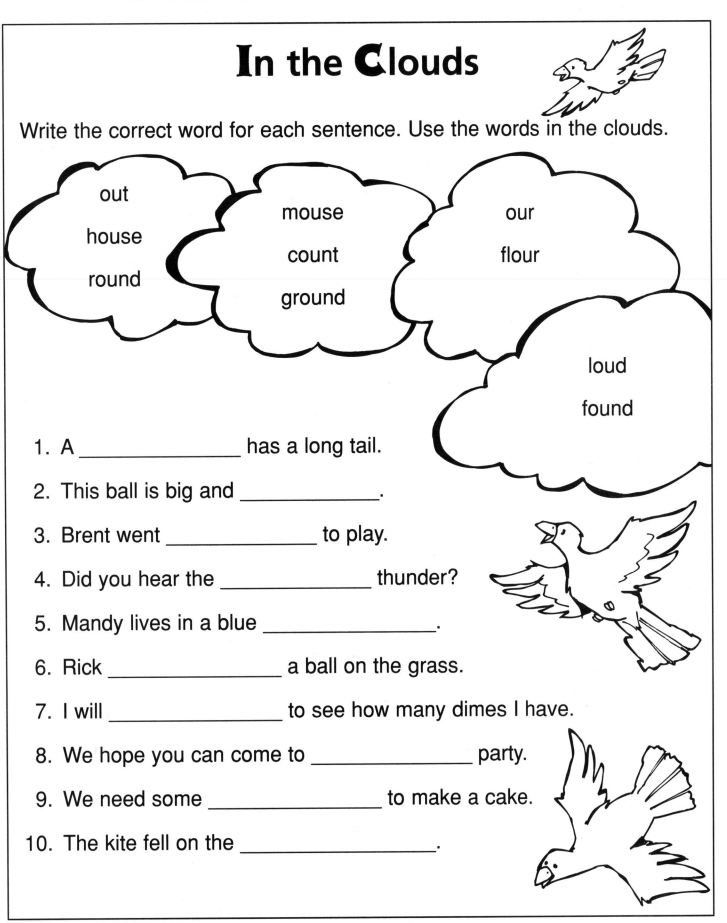

Write the correct word for each sentence. Use the words in the clouds.

out
house
round

mouse
count
ground

our
flour

loud
found

1. A _____ has a long tail.

2. This ball is big and _____.

3. Brent went _____ to play.

4. Did you hear the _____ thunder?

5. Mandy lives in a blue _____.

6. Rick _____ a ball on the grass.

7. I will _____ to see how many dimes I have.

8. We hope you can come to _____ party.

9. We need some _____ to make a cake.

10. The kite fell on the _____.

Going to Town

Help the family get from their house to the town. Circle the correct word for each picture. Write it on the line.

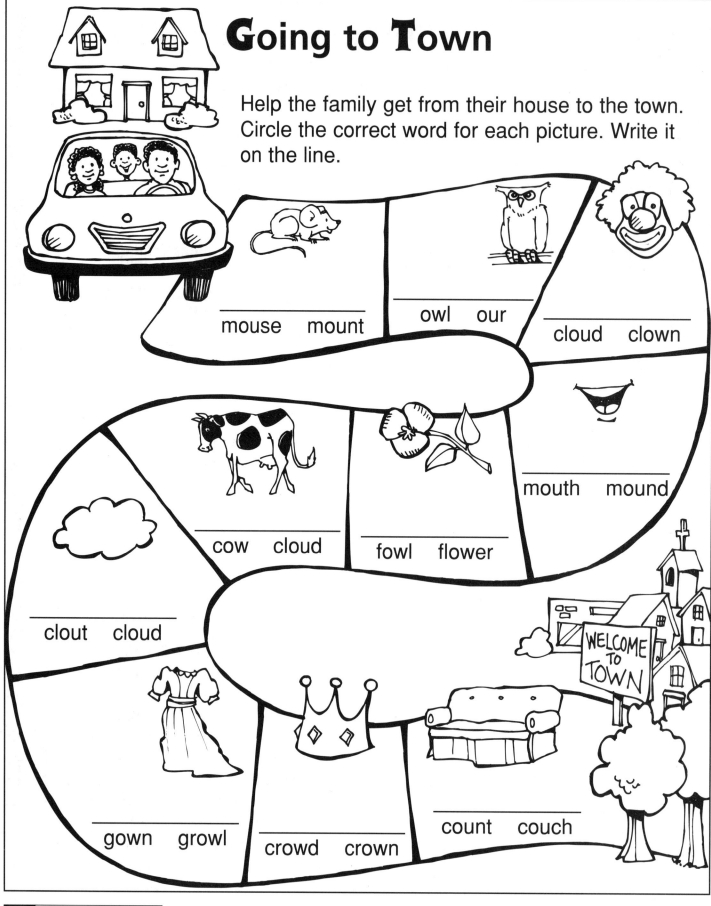

_____
mouse   mount

_____
owl   our

_____
cloud   clown

_____
mouth   mound

_____
cow   cloud

_____
fowl   flower

_____
clout   cloud

_____
gown   growl

_____
crowd   crown

_____
count   couch

WELCOME TO TOWN

FS123308 Phonics Made Simple—Grade 2 ■ © Frank Schaffer Publications, Inc.

Oo (room) and Oo (book)

A ROOMFUL OF "OO" WORDS   Class Activity

Bring to school several of the following items: a broom, a spoon, some tools, a pair of boots, a hoop, a spool of thread, a balloon, an ice cream scoop, and a stool. Have the students name each item as you list it on the board. Guide the class into seeing that each word contains *oo*. Then write other *oo* words on the board, and have the students read them aloud (examples: *cool, food, fool, mood, noon, pool, tooth*).

To check your students' auditory discrimination of *oo*, say pairs of words in which only one of the words in the pair contains *oo* (examples: *food, for; proud, poodle; goat, goose*). After you say each pair, have the students state which word has the *oo* sound.

LOOK AT AN "OO" RHYME   Class Activity

Write the following rhyme on the board, and have the class read it aloud:

> I have a great book.
> It helps you to cook.
> Just come take a look
> At my good cookbook!

Ask students to underline the words that rhyme. Have them notice that all these words contain *oo*. Help the children see that the *oo* in *book* has a shorter sound than the *oo* in *room*. To reinforce the *oo* sound as in *book*, say riddles such as the following, and have the class say and spell the answers:

This rhymes with *book*. It is something that is on the end of a fishing pole. (hook)

This rhymes with *good*. Some coats have this to keep your head warm. (hood)

This rhymes with *soot*. It is on the end of your leg. (foot)

Game

Beanbag Toss

Here's a fun game that reviews the two sounds of *oo*. Get enough beanbags so that you have one for each student. On each beanbag attach a piece of masking tape that has an *oo* word. Also get two buckets—one marked *room* and the other marked *book*. Set the buckets a few feet away from students. Then let the children take turns picking up a beanbag, reading the word on it, and throwing it in the corresponding bucket. (If you do not have enough beanbags, then attach two marked pieces of masking tape on opposite sides of each beanbag. One student can read one word on the beanbag before tossing; then the beanbag can be recycled and read by a different student.)

Balloon Fun

1.

Read the riddles. Write the answers on the balloons.
Use the words in the box.

| moon | zoo | broom | pool | goose |
| noon | roof | spoon | stool | school |

2.

3.

4.

1. You see this in the sky.

2. You can swim in this.

3. This is a tool for eating.

5.

4. You sweep with this.

5. You can see many animals here.

6.

6. Most people eat lunch at this time.

7. This has three legs.

7.

8. This is on the top of a house.

8.

9. This is a bird.

9.

10. You will see your teacher here.

10.

FS123308 Phonics Made Simple—Grade 2 ■ © Frank Schaffer Publications, Inc.

Lots of Books

Complete the sentences below. Use the words on the books.

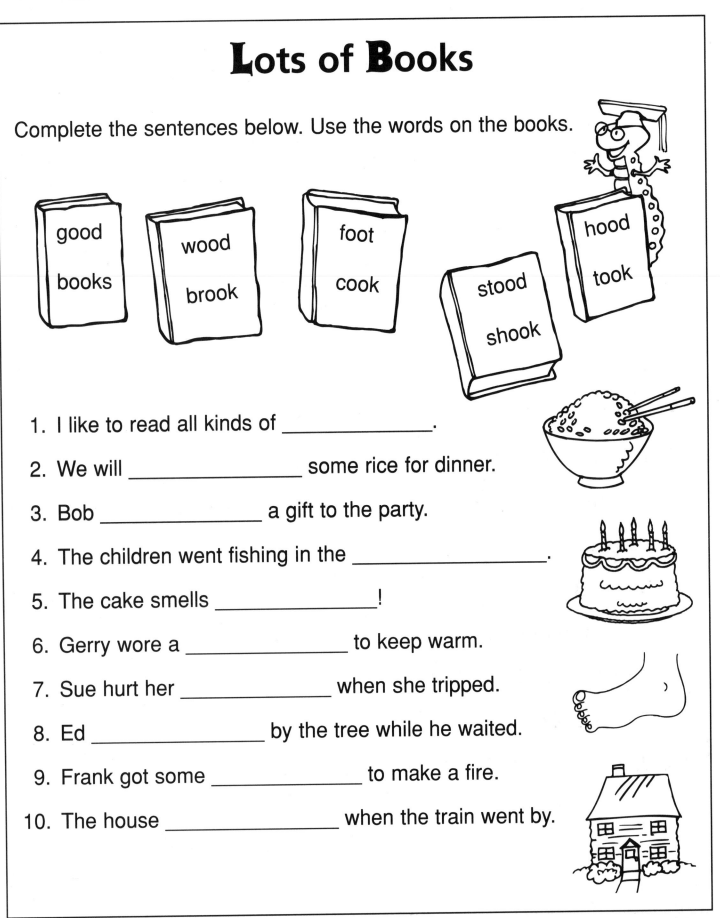

good
books

wood
brook

foot
cook

stood
shook

hood
took

1. I like to read all kinds of _____.

2. We will _____ some rice for dinner.

3. Bob _____ a gift to the party.

4. The children went fishing in the _____.

5. The cake smells _____!

6. Gerry wore a _____ to keep warm.

7. Sue hurt her _____ when she tripped.

8. Ed _____ by the tree while he waited.

9. Frank got some _____ to make a fire.

10. The house _____ when the train went by.

Good Foods

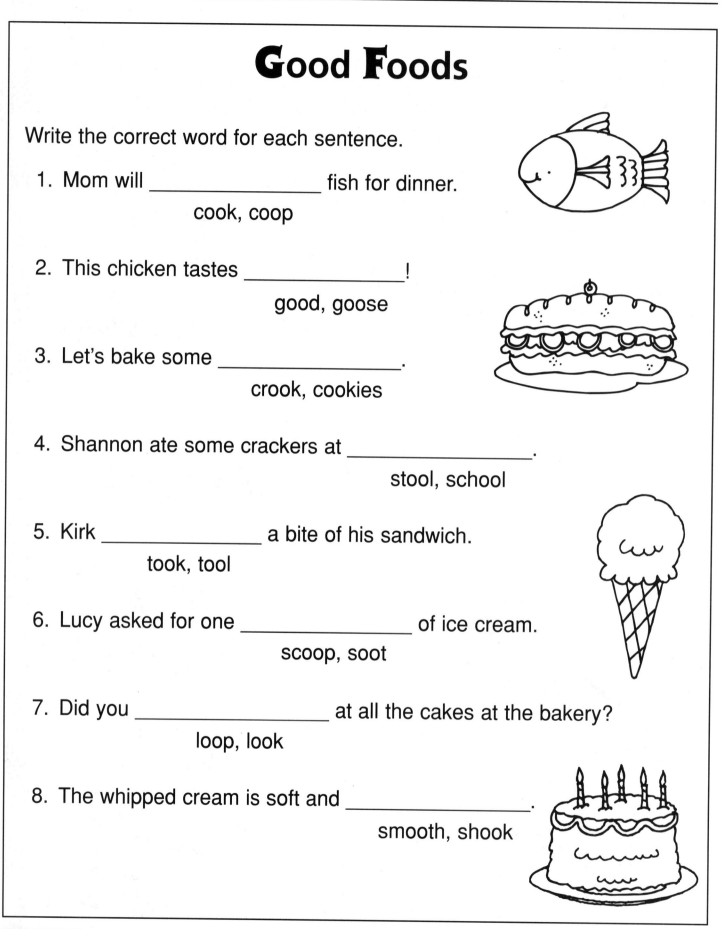

Write the correct word for each sentence.

1. Mom will _____ fish for dinner.
   cook, coop

2. This chicken tastes _____!
   good, goose

3. Let's bake some _____.
   crook, cookies

4. Shannon ate some crackers at _____.
   stool, school

5. Kirk _____ a bite of his sandwich.
   took, tool

6. Lucy asked for one _____ of ice cream.
   scoop, soot

7. Did you _____ at all the cakes at the bakery?
   loop, look

8. The whipped cream is soft and _____.
   smooth, shook

Oi and Oy

THE SAME SOUND—OI AND OY

Class Activity

Say these words to the class, and have the students point out what they hear in each one: *toy, boy, joy, annoy.* Write the words on the board, and have students underline the *oy* in each word. Next, say these

words and repeat the previous procedure: *coin, join, point, boil.* Have the class notice that the *oi* and *oy* make the same sound. Tell the students that usually *oy* appears at the end of a word and *oi* appears in the middle. Then write other *oi/oy* words on the board, and have the students read them aloud (examples: *coil, oil, noise, soil, enjoy, loyal, oyster*). For an extra challenge, have students use the words in sentences.

"OI" AND "OY" TONGUE TWISTERS

Class Activity

Words with *oi* and *oy* make challenging tongue twisters, and your students will enjoy creating some of their own. First, write the following sentence on the board: *Roy's oyster is annoyed by noise.* Then have student volunteers quickly say the sentence aloud three times.

Next, brainstorm with the students a list of *oi* and *oy* words they can use to make other tongue twisters. Write the words on the board. Then let the children use the words as a reference to write one or two tongue twisters. Later, let the students write their tongue twisters on chart paper so that the rest of the class can try saying them.

VOCABULARY CHALLENGE

Class Activity

Since there are not a lot of common words with *oi* and *oy*, you may want to enrich your students' vocabulary by introducing them to more challenging words. To do this, write the following questions on the board:

Does an <u>ointment</u> smell?

Is a <u>moist</u> towel wet or dry?

If you <u>hoist</u> a flag, does it go up or down?

When you <u>employ</u> somebody, do you hire or fire the person?

Would you find a <u>gargoyle</u> on clothing or on a building?

Have students look up the underlined words in a dictionary before answering each question. Later, ask students to define each of the *oi* and *oy* words.

Elroy's Coins

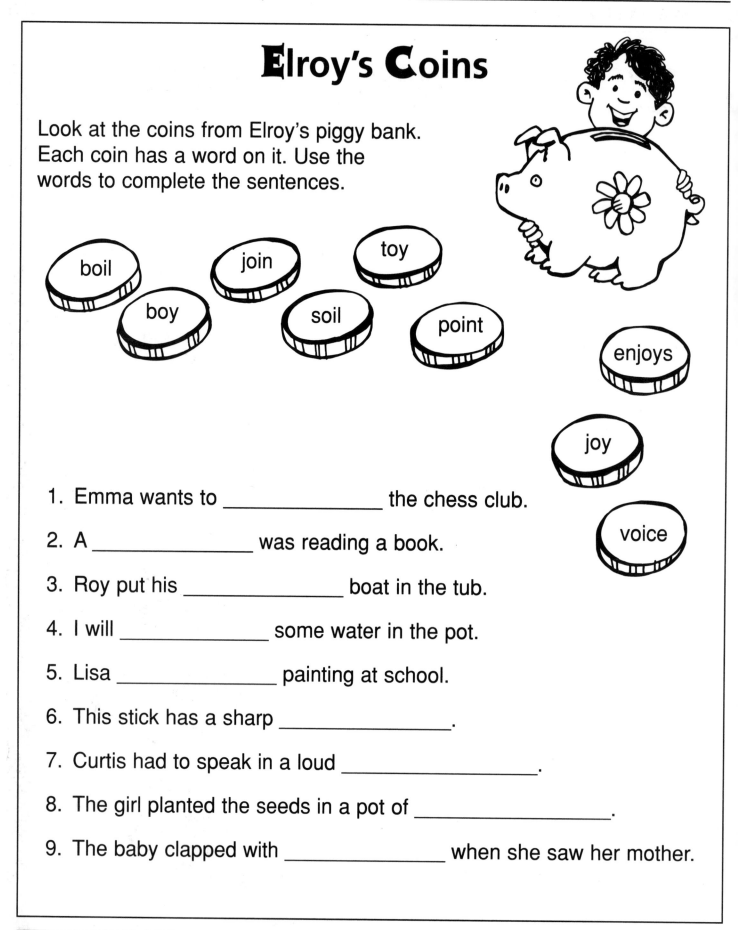

Look at the coins from Elroy's piggy bank.
Each coin has a word on it. Use the
words to complete the sentences.

boil

boy

join

soil

toy

point

enjoys

joy

voice

1. Emma wants to _____ the chess club.

2. A _____ was reading a book.

3. Roy put his _____ boat in the tub.

4. I will _____ some water in the pot.

5. Lisa _____ painting at school.

6. This stick has a sharp _____.

7. Curtis had to speak in a loud _____.

8. The girl planted the seeds in a pot of _____.

9. The baby clapped with _____ when she saw her mother.

FS123308 Phonics Made Simple—Grade 2 ▪ © Frank Schaffer Publications, Inc.

Au and Aw

A "SAD" SOUND—Au and Aw
Class Activity

Write these words on the board: *saw, law, draw, crawl.* Read the words to the students, and have them notice the sound that the *aw* makes. Tell the class that the *aw* sound is much like the noise we make when we are sad or disappointed.

Next, write these words on the board: *pause, autumn, auto,* and *because.* Read the words, and have the class notice that the same sound is produced by *au.* Then give students practice reading *aw* and *au* words by writing the following questions on the board: *Is there someone in class with an August birthday? Who taught you how to ride a bike? Have you ever caught a fish? What do you like to draw? What is one animal that crawls?* Call on students to read the questions aloud and underline the *aw/au* words. Then have students share their responses with one another.

ANIMAL FACTS
Class Activity

Use this writing activity to give students practice with *aw/au* words. First, list the following words on the board: *fawn, paw, claws, hawk, crawl, raw, jaw, autumn, because.* Divide the class into small groups, and have each group write at least five animal facts using the words listed. Let students look in encyclopedias or library books if they wish. Afterward, have the groups read their sentences to the class.

A fawn is a baby deer.

A cat has sharp claws.

A hawk hunts small animals.

Whales swim to the surface because they need to breathe air.

A lion has a powerful jaw.

ACT IT OUT
Class Activity

Write the following sentences one at a time on the board.

Crawl like a baby.

Give a big yawn.

Pretend you are drawing on the board.

Show how you would mow the lawn.

Show how a cat drinks from a saucer of milk.

Pretend you are hauling away a heavy load.

After you write a sentence, have the students read it and identify the *aw* or *au* word. Then have the class follow the directions and act out the various situations.

Paula's Schoolwork

Help Paula with her schoolwork.
Write the answer to each question.
Use the words in the box.

hawk	fawn	straw
saw	auto	yawn
draw	autumn	saucer

1. What cuts wood? _____

2. What is a baby deer? _____

3. What is another name for car? _____

4. What can you use to help you drink? _____

5. What bird is a good hunter? _____

6. What season comes after summer? _____

7. What is another word for dish? _____

8. What can you do with crayons? _____

9. What might you do if you are tired? _____

FS123308 Phonics Made Simple—Grade 2 ■ © Frank Schaffer Publications, Inc.

A SHORT VOWEL SOUND—Ea

Class Activity

Show the class a loaf of bread, a feather, a spool of thread, and a piece of leather. Write the corresponding *ea* words on the board, and have the students read them aloud. Have the class see that the *ea* in these words produce a short vowel sound. Then write other words (such as *ready*, *breath*, *heavy*, and *spread*) on the board. (At this point, you may wish to discuss the fact that words like *read* and *lead* can be read as either a long or short vowel word. Tell students that they will be able to figure out which way the word should be read when they see it used in context. In the sentence *I read a book yesterday*, for example, the *read* has a short *e* sound.)

For a follow-up activity, call on three or four students at a time to go to the board as you dictate a sentence to them. (Examples: *This lead pipe is heavy. Are you ready to go?*)

READ AND CLASSIFY

Class Activity

Get two sheets of chart paper. Write *ea as in eat* on one paper and *ea as in head* on the other. Then hand out to each child a flashcard on which you've written a word with *ea*. Have students read their words one at a time and tape them on the appropriate chart.

WHAT DID YOU DO?—Ew

Class Activity

Write the following sentences on the board: *Ken drew a picture. Nancy flew in a plane. Chris made some stew. Shannon threw a ball.* Have the class read the sentences and point out what the sentences have in common. (They all contain an *ew* word.) Ask student volunteers to underline the *ew* words in the sentences. Next, write other *ew* words on the board, and have the class write sentences with the words. For an extra challenge, tell students that the sentences must tell about what people did. (Examples: *Nina blew bubbles. Mrs. Burns read the newspaper. Stu renewed his library book.*)

Can You Figure It Out?

Use the words in the box to answer the riddles.

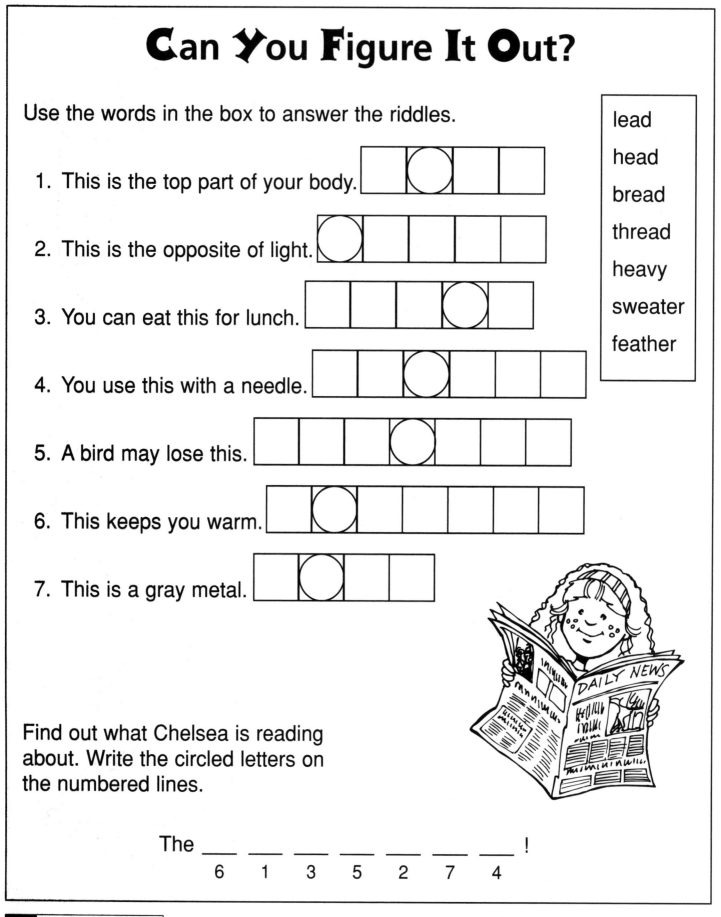

lead

head

bread

thread

heavy

sweater

feather

1. This is the top part of your body.

2. This is the opposite of light.

3. You can eat this for lunch.

4. You use this with a needle.

5. A bird may lose this.

6. This keeps you warm.

7. This is a gray metal.

Find out what Chelsea is reading about. Write the circled letters on the numbered lines.

The ___ ___ ___ ___ ___ ___ ___ !
     6   1   3   5   2   7   4

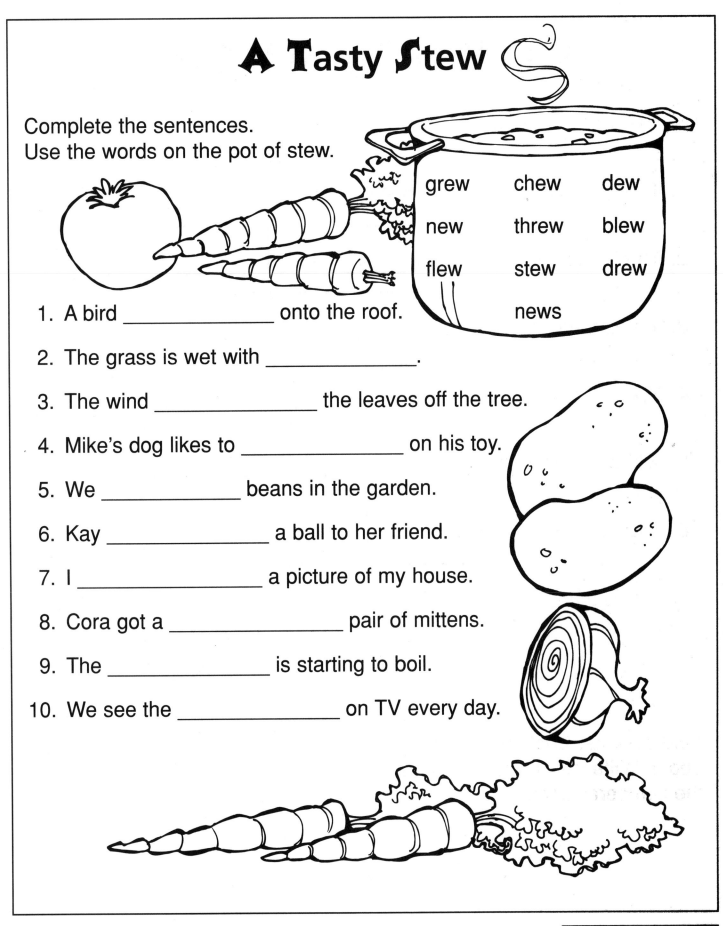

Name _____

A Tasty Stew

Complete the sentences.
Use the words on the pot of stew.

grew	chew	dew
new	threw	blew
flew	stew	drew
	news	

1. A bird _____ onto the roof.

2. The grass is wet with _____.

3. The wind _____ the leaves off the tree.

4. Mike's dog likes to _____ on his toy.

5. We _____ beans in the garden.

6. Kay _____ a ball to her friend.

7. I _____ a picture of my house.

8. Cora got a _____ pair of mittens.

9. The _____ is starting to boil.

10. We see the _____ on TV every day.

Tricky Vowels

Circle the word for each picture. Write it on the line.

foot fawn found _____	coin count cook _____	mow mouse moose _____
crew cloud crown _____	spoon spoil spout _____	toil town toys _____
threw thread trout _____	bow boil bowl _____	stew stood straw _____
brew boot boy _____	crow crawl crook _____	brown blow bread _____
saw sour soil _____	stood stool straw _____	head hook hawk _____

FS123308 Phonics Made Simple—Grade 2 ▪ © Frank Schaffer Publications, Inc.